Isaac D. Johnson

Counsel to Parents

And How to save the baby

Isaac D. Johnson

Counsel to Parents
And How to save the baby

ISBN/EAN: 9783337314620

Printed in Europe, USA, Canada, Australia, Japan

Cover: Foto ©Suzi / pixelio.de

More available books at **www.hansebooks.com**

COUNSEL TO PARENTS,

AND

How to Save the Baby.

BY

I. D. JOHNSON, M.D.,

AUTHOR OF "JOHNSON'S THERAPEUTIC KEY" AND OTHER MEDICAL WORKS.

KENNETT SQUARE, PA.
1889

Copyright, 1889, *I. D. Johnson, M.D.*,
Kennett Square, Pa.

TO
THE WOMAN'S CHRISTIAN TEMPERANCE UNION THIS
LITTLE VOLUME IS AFFECTIONATELY
DEDICATED
BY THE AUTHOR.

TO THE READER.

WE wish to say a few words in explanation of the motives that prompt us to write this little book. Its title sufficiently discloses the general nature of its contents, which it is unnecessary to particularize here. Suffice it to say that the subjects brought forth are of paramount importance, not only to parents, but to all classes of society, and especially to the *youth*, who, through ignorance of the information it imparts, are making wrecks of themselves, physically and mentally. It discusses the marital relations, points out the sin of sexual excesses, exposes the common vices of youth, and warns the offender of his impending doom. It treats these delicate but vital subjects in such a manner that the youth as well as the adult may read them with untold advantage, and be enabled to steer clear of the rocks and shoals upon which so many valuable lives have been wrecked.

The chief object, therefore, in preparing this work has been to give the reader some plain facts respecting the primary cause of disease and premature death, especially of the offspring. We are aware that we have imposed upon ourselves a responsible task, but we have studied the subject well and feel competent to give the needed advice to those who are willing to accept it. We have grown old in the service, having devoted nearly forty years of our life in studying the cause of the diseases and premature deaths which we daily witness around us; and we are satisfied that they are the direct result of the violation of the physiological laws, and which can and should be avoided. We write this little book, then, to give you the benefit of our observation and experience, trusting they will lead you to cherish still more the precious gifts which the Heavenly Father has intrusted to your care, and with the hope that there may be less sin, less suffering, more joy and a higher estimate placed upon the inestimable blessings of health. It is such a book as we would put into the hands of every parent—yes, into the hands of every girl and boy in the land old enough to understand and profit by its teachings.

The truth is, the people need a better knowledge of the laws of life and health, that they may live in such a manner as to avoid disease. Everybody is sick; the whole nation is suffering from a *nameless disease*, the infection of which has secretly crept into the veins and very marrow of our bones, sparing neither age, sex nor condition. All the doctors in Christendom cannot cure this "*disease without a name*" until the cause is removed. We must begin at first principles; we must be *rightly born*, and live in accordance with the laws of life; in other words, we must "cease to do evil and learn to do well."

We are aware that during the past few years a number of books have been written on this and kindred subjects, some of which are valuable and have done much good, others are unscientific, filled with dry details and technicalities such as only a professional reader can comprehend; while others are the devices of unscrupulous persons, written for the purpose of making money by their direct sale or by throwing out tempting baits for consultations or the sale of some favorite nostrum. We write from other motives, and with the happy thought that what we shall say will be the means by which thousands of men and women may preserve their own health and transmit as an inheritance to their children sound, vigorous constitutions. Then it will be that the painful and dangerous maladies that attack and destroy so many of our infants annually will be prevented, and the lives of these innocent little ones saved from a premature and untimely grave.

And now, my dear reader, all we ask of you is that, with the purest of motives and the love of truth in your heart, you will read and study the following pages, and, so far as the teachings they contain commend themselves to your judgment, that you accept and follow them faithfully, and we humbly trust that your life will become purer and sweeter as you accept the truths which are laid before you.

CONTENTS.

	Page.
To the Reader,	7
Chapter I.—Matrimonial,	11
" II.—Advice to Married People,	26
" III.—The Reproduction of Man,	42
" IV.—Pregnancy,	50
" V.—Hygienic Precautions During Pregnancy	57
" VI.—Diseases Incident to Pregnancy,	67
" VII.—Abortion—Miscarriage—Fœticide,	74
" VIII.—Labor—Parturition,	87
" IX.—How to Care for the Baby,	91
" X.—How to Save the Baby,	109
" XI.—How to Feed the Baby,	125
" XII.—Hand-Feeding of Babies,	135
" XIII.—The Early Education of Children,	149
The Evil Effects of Alcohol,	158
The Tobacco Habit,	177
The Opium Bondage,	186
" XIV.—Masturbation—Self-Abuse,	201
General Conclusions,	215

COUNSEL TO PARENTS,

AND

HOW TO SAVE THE BABY.

CHAPTER I.

MATRIMONIAL.

CANDIDATES FOR MATRIMONY—THE PASSION OF LOVE—
MENTAL AND PHYSICAL ADAPTATION—DISHONESTY
IN LOVE AFFAIRS—HINTS TO YOUNG WOMEN—HINTS
TO YOUNG MEN, ETC., ETC.

THE subject of marriage is not a theme for special consideration in this little volume. Neither time nor space will permit us to enter into any extended discussion of it here. We have only a few thoughtful words to offer the candidates of matrimony as a prelude to what is to follow in the discussion of the subject that adorns the title-page. And as we are about to consider the primary cause of disease which leads to premature death, we invite to our counsel all those who contemplate entering the sacred relations of marriage, that we may reason together and find out, if possible, what part married people—and especially *parents*—act in the great drama of human life, as it relates to the production of disease and premature death in the offspring.

Health is the greatest blessing ever vouchsafed to man. It is the basis of all human happiness, progress and reform. Unfortunately for mankind we are all suffering "for the sin of being sick;" the nations of the earth are diseased, dying prematurely. What the people want is *health;* and if we are ever to obtain it the work must begin at home with each individual. Every man and woman who lives in the conditions of health, and avoids the causes of disease, helps to make the race better; and if such persons would combine their purified lives in the production of *healthy* offspring, they would do a noble work for the redemption of humanity. "There is no disease without a cause, and the cause is closely related to the remedy." In the following pages we wish to show what this remedy is, and how to apply it.

THE PASSION OF LOVE.—What is this passion of love that reigns in the soul of man, that inspires in him such gallant respect for woman, and in woman such tender regard for man? Is it mere affection, or friendship, that magnetizes, as it were, with a thrill of delight, and makes the lips cling together in dewy kisses of inexpressible rapture at the mere touch of the hand? As young men and women approach the years of maturity they become conscious of a new and strong attachment for each other, unlike that experienced in their early school-days. When this attraction or magnetic influence exists in a strong degree between one man and one woman, and is reciprocal, it is called love, and by common consent is made an essential condition of marriage. Such attraction is based on the sexual nature, which begins at the age of puberty, and which creates wants that must be met before the fullest development of persons can be attained. Sexual passion, then —which is a legitimate and component part of love—exerts no small share in "the tie that binds" in the marriage relations; indeed, so closely connected is it with what we call love, that it is impossible to tell where one ends and the other begins; therefore, those who are qualified to confer on each other this *summum bonum* of matrimonial felicity are bound together by the strongest bonds of union connected with our nature.

"Marriage, then," says Mrs. Shepherd, "is the heaven-ordained way for men and women to associate, so that all the longings and needs of their whole being may be gratified. For people have an instinctive sense that not only the physical nature, but even the intellectual and spiritual elements of the soul will flourish best in the companionship of one chosen and cherished above all others of the sex. In a perfect union this will be the case. What one lacks in character the other will supply."

MENTAL AND PHYSICAL ADAPTATION.—And now a few suggestions to the candidates for matrimony. One of the most important matters to be considered in forming a matrimonial alliance is for the parties to secure entire mental and physical adaptation. If we study the mental constitution of man, we find it composed of moral, intellectual and perceptive faculties; these distinguish him from all others of the animal creation. Woman possesses the same mental faculties as man, but in a subordinate degree. In man the intellectual faculties predominate, in woman the affectional. It is said man reaches conclusions through the process of reasoning, woman by intuition. Man acts from reasoning or through the understanding, woman from impulse or affection. Men and women differ mentally as well as physically in many respects. Some men have stronger affections than some women, and some women have stronger intellects than some men.

Man physically is superior to woman in all that constitutes manhood, whereas woman is superior to man in all that constitutes womanhood, so that neither, mentally nor physically, can claim superiority over the other. This is as it should be, for we find all things created with relation of perfect fitness or harmony to nature; and if we only obey the laws of our being, we will have health and happiness as a reward of well-doing. A true marriage is capable of yielding the highest degree of happiness, and such a harmonious relationship can only exist between persons of similar endowments, and not between those of opposites. Mental adaptation in marriage consists in, at least, an approximate correspondence of the mental faculties. A man with large intellectual faculties should never be united to a woman with equal or superior intellect, for in that case she will neither admire nor appreciate his wisdom. No wife can respect a husband who is her inferior, and without respect there can be no love. Nor can an intelligent husband enjoy the society of a wife who is ignorant or of feeble intellect. And for similar reasons a man with very strong affections should not marry a woman with feeble affections, for in that case the man will neither appreciate nor reciprocate her love. So it seems certain that where the union between the sexes is to be a happy one, the affection should be the strongest on the side of the woman, and where the intellect is to decide the matter, the preponderance should be on the side of the man. As to the moral faculties, they should be about equal in each, for the possession of high religious sentiments by one, and a total destitution of them in the other, is a frequent cause of matrimonial discords; for a devoted husband will cease to love a wife who neither sympathizes with nor participates in his religious sentiments. On the other hand, if two persons marry who have large combativeness, there will be domestic strife and discord where peace should reign supreme. Then, again, if both should possess a predominant love for ruling others, it is plain to be seen what a conflict there would be when the actors undertook to exercise their rightful prerogatives with each other. Or, let two be wedded whose ruling passion is love of money, and their desire for gain will grow stronger and stronger each day, and with its acquisition will come an endless struggle for its possession, which they must soon leave for interested relatives to quarrel over. And so it is with all the evil passions which are predominant in both: they will strengthen in each other as time goes on, and, beside the unhappy results which accrue to the parties themselves, still more disastrous must be the evil tendencies transmitted to their offspring. But if those of opposite or different passions come together, then there will be frequent dissensions and family jars; but the tendency will be rather to restrain than strengthen the predominant passions; and, however unpleasant or painful this want of harmony may be, it is far better than the marriage of those in whom the evil passions are similar. Therefore, if the great ends of marriage—which are the present and future happiness of man, and the perpetuation of the race—are to be fulfilled, it is of infinite importance that all those who purpose entering the bonds of matrimony should secure, if possible, entire mental and physical adaptation in reference to these objects. And at the expense of repetition we would say that a man with strong intellectual faculties should marry a woman with correspondingly strong mental endowments; that a man with strong affections should choose for his wife one with equal or even stronger affections. And a man with strong animal passions should never marry a woman with equally strong animal passions; and in no case should he take for his wife a weak, delicate woman, for reasons given elsewhere. On the other hand, persons with evil passions predominating should never unite in wedlock with those of similar passions, but with opposites. A young woman should not forget that her lover virtually proposes himself as the future father of her children; only from this standpoint can she make an intelligent and safe estimate of him.

PHYSICAL ADAPTATION.—In regard to the physical qualifications of candidates for the hymeneal altar, it will be better for the present and future good of the human race if large and well-formed men would select for companions women of a proportionate size. And, for a similar reason, it will be better for a small man and a large woman, or a large man and a small woman, to unite in marriage, so that the size and strength of the one may make up for the diminutiveness and weakness of the other; but the disparity in size should not be great. For it must be evident to all that these conditions will have a direct bearing on the mental and physical development of the future offspring; and if we would transmit to posterity a noble race of men and women, we must comply with the laws of procreation. We cannot expect strong, vigorous, healthy children from weak, dwarfish or deformed parents. The farmer does not expect good corn or wheat if he sows a poor quality of seed; nor does he expect to raise good cows and sheep from a poor, diminutive breed, or a beautiful fleet horse from an inferior stock. And as man is an animal he is subject to all the laws of hereditary descent which govern the propagation of other animals. So, diseased parents beget diseased children, and through them it is handed down to the third and fourth generation. But with good conditions and surroundings the mistakes and diseases of birth may be gradually eradicated, and children born ugly, diseased, and with unfortunate mental and moral tendencies, may become beautiful, healthy and good.

It is hardly necessary to define more specifically the mental and physical adaptation in marriage; very few will follow advice in regard to this matter; the emotions carry the individuals away, and reason loses all control. Let all young persons, therefore, be exceedingly careful how they allow emotional excitement to gain the ascendancy.

DISHONESTY IN LOVE AFFAIRS.—Having briefly considered the question of mental and physical adaptation in marriage, we come to speak of another matter that is closely related to our subject, and one that should interest all who are seeking matrimonial felicity. We refer to the matter of dishonesty practiced among young people in their love affairs. Too many, in conducting their courtships, practice all manner of deceptions to entrap each other. If the young lady be religious, her admiring friend will attend church regularly and go through all the forms of worship; if she is of a literary turn of mind, he takes to books and study; if she is opposed to the use of tobacco, he temporarily discards the "filthy weed;" if she takes snuff, he does the sneezing. If his form is ugly, crooked or ill-shaped, he bribes the tailor to conceal the defects. If nature has failed in developing her womanly charms, then cotton and whalebone, powder and paint make up for the deficiency. Many a man has married what he supposed was an armful of female loveliness, which proved to be little more than a bundle of dry-goods.

Thus is every form of device resorted to in courtship to cover up the mental and physical defects, which must sooner or later be exposed after marriage. Men and women should no more deceive each other in love affairs than in the affairs of business. If they do so, then they are swindlers and cheats, which the parties will come to realize when it is too late. Honesty is the best policy, not only in love affairs, but in all the transactions of human life. For a young man to gain the affections of a young lady, or a young lady to gain the affections of a young man by false pretenses, is no less a crime than obtaining money by similar means, and the act should be made an indictable offense at common law, and the perpetrator punished accordingly. This would put a stop to rascals becoming the husbands of virtuous women, and female tricksters from taking advantage of honest men. When men and women come to realize the importance of dealing frankly and honestly with each other, then will a real, genuine reform be inaugurated in all the relations of life.

MARRYING FOR WEALTH.— Again, parents or relatives often instigate matrimonial unions from false and selfish motives. Persons forming such an alliance under these circumstances are seldom so fortunate as to get congenial companions. Men will sometimes marry those for whom they possess not one spark of affection, in order to secure wealth. And women will often accept the proposals of rich men for whom they hardly feel common respect, thinking that a luxurious home and glittering gold will compensate for the misery they will have to encounter from an odious husband. No greater delusion can be entertained than that riches alone can make persons happy in matrimony. True marriage is not a trap in which people are caught, nor a Bastile in which they are confined. It is a condition of mutual attraction in absolute freedom, and not one that can be purchased with silver or gold. Hence, marrying for a home, or to please parents or friends, seldom leads to a true spiritual union, where peace, contentment and harmony should reign, but often subjects the parties to a slavery the most abject. Two persons may swear eternal love to each other upon a "stack of Bibles" as high as a house, but if they do not love each other, they have no right to expect that peace and happiness which grow out of the spiritual union of two loving souls. Without a strict observance of the laws of natural attraction that should exist between the parties, it will be far better for humanity, and the innocent offspring of remote posterity, if such persons would consent to remain in a state of single blessedness. And now, in negotiating a life partnership, let me give a few

HINTS TO YOUNG WOMEN.—Let no young woman accept the heart and hand of a young man who uses *alcoholic liquors* in any form, or *tobacco*. We can imagine nothing more pitiful than a young woman being led to the marriage altar by a young man who is addicted to the use of intoxicating liquors; the chances are ten to one that she will drag out a miserable and unhappy existence, and finally die a drunkard's broken-hearted wife.

Shun the young man who uses tobacco; if he does not already drink intoxicating liquors, he is almost certain to do so, for it is a well-known fact that nine-tenths of all who use tobacco use alcoholic stimulants to a greater or less extent; while among those who *abstain* from the use of tobacco not one in fifty uses alcoholic beverages.

This is a grave matter for a young woman to consider before entering into a life-partnership with a young man. For a clean, pure, loving woman to marry a man who is addicted to the dirty, filthy practice of smoking or chewing tobacco is contrary to all her natural and womanly instincts. No man would think of marrying a woman who uses tobacco, or intoxicating liquors, or profane language, or who was a gambler or a licentious woman! Yet women very often marry men, with a full knowledge of all these facts, regarding them as a necessary element of man's nature.

Do not marry a *lustful* man, or you will have cause to regret it. If his approaches towards you indicate that he is that kind of a fellow, do not consent to become his wife; if you do, you will have a domestic trouble on your hands that will last nearly as long as he lives.

Never marry an *invalid*, or a man who inherits the taint of insanity, consumption, cancer, epilepsy or scrofula; if you do, your children will inherit and suffer from the same diseases, and you will find him a poor arm of support when the strain of life comes.

Never marry a *close-fisted*, niggardly man; if you do, you will be afflicted the balance of your natural life. He will "stint you in everything," and make you "beg for every cent of money you get" that comes through your joint-earnings.

Never marry a "*dude*," or a young man who drives a fast horse and carries a long whip; he will never amount to much, except during the honeymoon; after that he will begin to wane and finally turn out a failure.

Never marry a man under *twenty-three* or *twenty-four* years of age, and don't let him marry you until you are *over* twenty. Children begotten by fathers between the ages of 25 and 40 years are the most robust; this is also true of those born of mothers between the ages of 20 and 30 years.

HINTS TO YOUNG MEN. — On the other hand, let no young man select for his wife a young woman with a temperament *very similar* to his own; it should be different from his in all leading characteristics. The shape of her head as well as her body should be different from yours.

Never marry a woman with a *small waist;* you will entail upon your offspring not only ill health, but deformity which will descend to future posterity.

Never marry a pale, delicate woman; if you do, you will regret it all your life. You will have her to watch and to nurse, instead of having her as a helpmate; and, besides, your children, if they live, will grow up weakly, sickly mortals, and never enjoy health.

Never select a wife from a family that is tainted with epilepsy, insanity or consumption. These diseases are almost certain to develop in the wife and descend to her children as a legacy.

And, finally, never marry a woman without first telling her everything you know about yourself, and what your aims and aspirations are. Be perfectly frank and honest with her; do not deceive her under any circumstances. She will find you out after the wedding, and if you have taken advantage of her, she will never have *entire confidence* in you thereafter. If you cannot do this, just be frank enough to say to her that your character is such that you are unworthy to become her husband, and that she must forgive your shortcomings, and then, without repugnance of conscience, bid her farewell.

CHAPTER II.

ADVICE TO MARRIED PEOPLE.

THE MATRIMONIAL VOYAGE—A FEW SUGGESTIONS—INTERESTS RECIPROCAL—INDIFFERENCE—THE VALUE OF A SMILE—DECEPTION—ABUSE OF THE SEXUAL FUNCTIONS—WHAT CONSTITUTES ABUSE—CAUSE OF DISEASE—ENTIRE CONTINENCE.

HAVING in the previous article made a few suggestions for the benefit of those who were candidates for marriage, we wish to devote a brief space to the consideration of that other class of individuals who, having "taken each other for better or worse," and having pledged themselves to mutual fidelity and love, are about to start on their matrimonial journey of life.

And now, right at the threshold, at the very beginning, let me whisper in your ears a few words which, if fairly recognized, will be of inestimable advantage to you. We will suppose that you have gone through a happy courtship; that you have stood up amid friends and flowers and made a solemn promise to love and protect each other; that you have received the congratulations of friends and the prayers of loving parents. Now, after this is all over, and you have retired to your chamber to meditate and talk over your future prospects in life, and the happy moments you have spent together, and how much you love each other, remember that this love which you bear to each other, and which you should prize above everything else in this world, will gradually disappear if you give yourself up to *unrestrained sexual indulgence.* And also remember that you must not only avoid excesses, but you must *preserve* that *chastity* and *respect* for each other that have hitherto characterized your behavior during courtship. A countless host of young married people turn their love into indifference through their ignorance in regard to these matters.

Again, we would suggest another little matter which you will find of great practical importance as you journey along through life: have a little drawer in your secretary or bureau in which to keep your money; have a good lock on it supplied with two keys—one for each of you—and let it be fairly understood that either party shall have the same right and privilege to use this money as the other. This little arrangement will prevent a great deal of trouble between you, and will increase your mutual confidence and love for each other.

Interests Reciprocal.—The interests of husband and wife are so interwoven that whatever effects one is sure to effect the other. Wives especially have been advised as to what their duty is, while husbands have been much neglected in this particular. It will be well for both to read the marriage ceremony once in a while to see if they live up to the promise made to love, obey and cherish each other. It is far too common for husbands to think if they provide money generously for their wives that they have done their whole duty. But there is something besides money that is necessary to make the home what it should be—a center of peace and happiness. We also hear much said about the influence of women in the home, which no one will underrate; but, says a writer: "The husband is to the home what the sun is to the natural world, and we all know what a difference it makes whether the sun shines out bright and clear, or is cloudy. We can scarcely rise above the depressing influence of darkened skies, and no family can rise above the gloom that falls on it when the face of the father and husband is turned in darkness away from it. I know that a man's business is often harassing, and in the world he gets many rough jostlings, and he ought to have everything serene and sweet at home; and every true wife will accord it. But if he meets vexations and perplexities in his business, that gives him no right to come home ill-natured and gloomy. His wife may have had an equally trying day at home. If he comes home bright and cheery, and she, forgetting her troubles, meets him in the same spirit, how much better than for both to be despondent and ill-humored. Dear friends, try the sunshine. It will be reflected back into your own lives, making each day glad. Few husbands realize how much their wives value praise and commendation from their husbands' lips, how by appreciative words the wife's cares and trials are lightened and her burdens made easy to bear. Life holds no sorrows that can hurt very much if full love and confidence exist between husband and wife. The wife should know about her husband's business; it will guide her in her expenditures and will strengthen the bonds of sympathy.

"Indifference is the deadly rust of married life. It should never be allowed to get a foothold in the home. As we keep our silver bright by constant polishing, and our cutlery by constant scouring, so should we take pains to keep ourselves bright and fresh for each other, and practice all the innocent social arts that made the period of courtship so delightful. For whom should the husband make himself interesting and attractive, but for the being nearest to him on earth? On whom should the wife lavish blandishments and fascinations, if not on her husband?"

THE VALUE OF A SMILE.—Beside sunshine, who can tell the value of a smile? It costs the giver nothing, but is beyond price to the erring and relenting, the sad and cheerless, the lost and forsaken. It disarms malice, subdues temper, turns hatred to love, revenge to kindness, and paves the darkest paths with gems of sunlight. A smile on the brow betrays a kind heart, a pleasant friend, an affectionate mother, a dutiful son, a happy husband. It adds a charm to beauty, and it decorates the face of even the most deformed.

DECEPTION.—Another matter worthy of consideration is the necessity of starting with and maintaining perfect confidence in each other. No deception whatever should be allowed to exist between husband and wife; every thought and deed should be made known to each other. The husband should entertain no secrets or business transactions that he is not willing to confide to his wife. And if the wife has any secrets "locked up in her heart" that she "would not have her husband know for the world," the sooner she ventilates the matter the better it will be for all concerned. It always strengthens the confidence in each other when a confession is made of any injustice or wrong committed by one against the other. On the other hand, anything hidden or concealed by one, though never discovered by the other, is sure to breed discontent sooner or later, because it is a peculiarity of the human mind to suspect in others what we are guilty of ourselves. And whenever husband or wife detects any deception in each other, it is about time to take an account of stock, and prepare to divide the household goods; then, bidding each other good-bye, one starting in the direction of the rising, and the other towards the setting sun, make haste to get as far apart as possible, burning all bridges in the rear; for it will be impossible to restore confidence when deceit and dishonesty have had a hiding-place in the bosom of either. Therefore, if the matrimonial voyage is to be a pleasant and happy one, if husband and wife are to journey along together through life, and enjoy the blessings that come only from two loving hearts, then they must be just to themselves, to their neighbor, and to all mankind. For, remember, all that is base and mean and miserable comes from a disregard of the principles enunciated in the golden rule, that whatsoever ye would that others should do unto you, do ye also unto them.

ABUSES OF THE SEXUAL FUNCTION.—A delicate subject, truly, but one we cannot afford to overlook, as it has a direct bearing on the subject under consideration. By many the marriage vow seems to be regarded as equivalent to the largest license for an unlimited indulgence of the animal propensity. The evils which result from such indulgence are liable to be overlooked even by the parties themselves, but they are well known by every physician of common experience. The husband frequently suffers from general debility, weakness and pain in the back, cramps, dyspepsia, impotency and a tendency to epileptic seizures, etc. And an evil of no small account is the *steady growth* of the sexual passion from a want of proper restraint in this direction. In this way the habitual yielding to inclination often determines the life-long behavior of the parties concerned. Much harm to both sexes has resulted from the widespread teaching that the passion of men is by nature stronger than that of women. It has led millions of men to feel justified in gratifying lust, under the name of passion, at any cost, sacrifice or suffering to their victims both within the marriage pale and outside of it.

But the chief sufferers from the abuse of this function are the wives and innocent offspring.

Nearly all medical writers agree that one of the most common causes of uterine derangement and female weakness to which married women are subject comes from excessive cohabitation. Thousands of these unfortunate wives are constantly under the doctor's care for the treatment of local ailments which have their sole origin in sexual excesses, for which their husbands are responsible. The diseases known as inflammation and ulceration of the womb, prolapsus, leucorrhœa, deranged menstruation, dysmenorrhœa, miscarriage, hysteria and an endless train of sympathetic nervous affections are among the number attributed to this cause. Not that men and women may not suffer from all these diseases where no such excesses have been indulged, but they are much more liable to occur where these excesses have been committed. The gratification, then, of this passion—or any other beyond its legitimate end—is always attended with serious results. The process is undoubtedly one of the most exhausting and draws more heavily upon the vitality of man and woman than any other of the animal functions. And the delicate husband or wife who indulges in this gratification to any great extent will necessarily have to suffer in consequence, for they seldom have any strength to expend in that direction.

O. S. Fowler, who is excellent authority on this subject, says: "Many a husband has buried more wives than one, *killed* outright, ignorantly yet effectually, by the brutality of his passion. Reader, if thou knowest none such thou knowest not the *cause* of all the deaths that transpire around thee! And yet the pulpit, the press, the lecture-room are silent in view of this vast, this wicked waste of life."

But it is not the husband and wife alone who suffer from this abuse. If it were it would be, comparatively speaking, of little consequence; but it is the innocent offspring and society at large that are the chief sufferers. And if we are ever to have a strong, vigorous, healthy offspring, free from the taint of disease and out of which to construct a noble race of men and women, then we must look to the *parents* to give us such, for the first condition of health to every organized being is to be well born.

Without this prerequisite we shall continue to have a poor, weak, sickly, short-lived and suffering offspring. For it must be borne in mind that the seeds of disease are sown in the mother's womb.

In the act of reproduction the seminal fluid is furnished by the male, and the ova or germ is supplied by the female; when these constituents come together they form the rudiments of the fœtus or future human being. Now, any unhealthy condition of the male will affect the seminal fluid; if he has exhausted his vitality by the abuse of the sexual passions; if he has poisoned his system by the use of narcotic stimulants, rum or tobacco, then he cannot beget a healthy child. If the female is diseased, or is the victim of any vice that lowers her standard of health or has dwarfed her body, then she is unable to furnish the life-germ for healthy offspring. A "corrupt tree cannot bring forth good fruit;" neither can diseased parents bring forth healthy children. Until we come to understand the laws of hereditary transmission, and strive to avoid the causes of disease, we must continue to "suffer for the sin of being sick." Humanity lies groaning under the accumulated errors of ages, and these have been handed down to us as an inheritance by our progenitors, until the very life-blood of the nation has become polluted, and we are threatened on all sides with disease and premature death. Now, every man and woman who lives in the conditions of health, and who avoids the causes of disease, helps the race; and if such persons would combine their efforts in the production of a healthy offspring, they would achieve a noble work for the redemption and purification of humanity.

WHAT CONSTITUTES AN ABUSE OF THE ANIMAL PASSION?—This question will naturally arise in the mind of every thoughtful person. It is one of vital importance and deserving serious consideration.

The relation of husband and wife is essentially one of purity and use; if either person seeks simply the selfish gratification of passion, without regard to the health and happiness of the other or desire for children, it becomes sensual. Marriage should never be regarded as a condition granting license to the passions. The reproduction of human life is certainly a legitimate use for the gratification of the sexual function, but when indulged to excess from mere passionate enjoyment it becomes an evil of fearful magnitude. The question is not what is pleasurable, or what is an excess, but what is *right* and *useful*. The lower animals, not gifted with erring reason, but with unerring instinct, and not having the liberty of choice between good and evil, cohabit only at stated periods, when pleasure and reproduction are alike possible. Would that we could say as much for man! With all his intellect and reasoning powers, he is a slave to his passions, and too often enters the marriage relations as an excuse for free indulgence. Such persons would have us believe they are acting according to their natural propensities; but man's nature is *perverted*, and therefore cannot be relied upon as a safe guide.

Many eminent writers contend that temperate indulgence tends to strengthen the bonds which unite husband and wife, and adds to their health and happiness; while others, equally eminent, among whom are some of our most distinguished physiologists and medical observers, agree that " intercourse not intended to be fruitful is unhallowed, and, if meant to be unfruitful, is licentious, whether had in or out of wedlock;" and that there is but one way to guard against sexual excess, and that is *non-intercourse except for the production of offspring.* This may seem at first thought like the prohibition of a legitimate pleasure, and some will say they might as well live bachelors or old maids; but when we come to understand the intent of the laws of this department of our being, we shall find it is the only *safe* and *right* road that leads to *health* and *happiness.*

The whole human family is sick; wherever we go or look we find men and women suffering from a *nameless* disease. It is especially noticeable among *married* people. They look careworn, are pale, listless, depressed in spirits, are irritable, have poor appetites and bad memories; they have *weak eyes* and are obliged to wear glasses even while young in years; they suffer from headache, indigestion, and have frequent moody spells. They are not exactly sick, but always complaining, and have an aversion to all kinds of employment. This *"disease without a name"* is transmitted to the innocent offspring who come into the world with weak, delicate constitutions, one-third of whom die before they reach their second birthday, while those who survive grow up with enfeebled bodies and sensual appetites to perpetuate this *disease without a name* through future generations. Every city, town and country village is full of men and women who are victims of this *disease without a name.* They take all manner of drugs, nostrums and quack medicines, "nerve-tonics," "bitters," "iron," "blood-purifiers," etc. Doctors far and near are consulted, but to little or no purpose, and thousands of these victims go down to the grave annually, while their nearest relatives and most intimate friends know not the cause of their early decay and premature death.

Now, there is a *cause* for this " *disease without a name,*" and that cause is *excessive sexual indulgence.* The abuse of this passion has been the besetting sin in all ages, and to-day it threatens the very existence of our race. There is but one way to cure this disease, and that is to stop the *producing* cause. Most women and many men can do this if they will. What the people want is to be enlightened on this subject, to be made aware of the terrible consequences which result from an abuse of the sexual functions. The errors which have been generated in the past can only be counteracted by educating the young on sexual ethics, and a general dissemination of knowledge on the normal functions and rational uses of the generative organs. Ignorance is the active agent of all evil, and especially is this the case in regard to the marital relations.

ENTIRE CONTINENCE.—A very erroneous idea prevails among some that continence is injurious to health, giving rise to a diseased condition. Some physicians have taught this, and books have been written in support of the theory. The assumption is that the *seminal fluid* is analogous to bile, gastric juice, saliva and other glandular secretions, which, when once formed, must be used and expelled from the system. The logical deduction from this theory is, that men or boys after the age of puberty, to maintain the standard of health, must expel the *seminal* fluid at certain periods, either by sexual intercourse or by masturbation. Such a theory is not only erroneous, but is repugnant to the moral and finer sensibilities of human nature. It affords the immoral a ready excuse for their debauchery, and "turns the heaven of the affections into a hell of the passions, which is fast destroying the vitality and happiness of our race." There can be no doubt that a total abstinence from sexual indulgence is compatible with a healthy state of the body. The highest medical authorities agree that no disease or tendency to any disease results from entire continence. And while vital statistics prove that the average duration of life is greater among married than among single, yet it is more than probable that this is due to other causes than those under consideration. As a general rule, the habits of married people are more uniform and temperate than the unmarried; they are less exposed, better contented and happier—all of which are sufficient to account for the difference in longevity.

In our present unnatural condition, continence would seem to be almost impossible: but, with the love of truth and a determination to do right, we are convinced that there is not an unruly passion or morbid fancy which may not be controlled. The first step in the right direction to accomplish this is to occupy the mind with pure thoughts and noble sentiments; to avoid all sensual excitation, and the reading of sentimental and immoral romances which tend to excite the animal passions. Living an honest, sober, industrious life will do much to appease the venereal appetite, and sustain our efforts in getting rid of bad habits. Persons who have not already given way to improper indulgences will find little difficulty in restraining themselves, if they will properly restrain their thoughts and avoid the use of stimulants, narcotics, tea, coffee and tobacco. By pursuing this course they will soon find their desires growing less and their passions much more easily controlled.

An important matter of hygiene and true living is separate beds for children as well as adults, married and single; it puts temptation somewhat out of the way of the easily tempted, and, besides, it is more conducive to health. (See CRIMINAL ABORTION).

CHAPTER III.

THE REPRODUCTION OF MAN.

CONCEPTION—THE MALE AND FEMALE PRINCIPLE WHICH UNITES TO FORM A NEW BEING—CONDITIONS NECESSARY TO INSURE HEALTHY OFFSPRING—PRIMARY CAUSE OF DISEASE—FŒTAL DEVELOPMENT, ETC.

CONCEPTION.—As stated in a previous article, conception takes place by the male sperm coming in positive contact with the ova or *germ-cells* furnished by the generative organs of the female, so that a new being results. This sublime function is performed by the two male and female organs, the testes and the ovaries. The spermatic fluid, which is secreted by the testicles, is a whitish viscid fluid that resembles the white of egg and contains numerous small cells called *sperm-cells* or spermatozoa. The ova or ovules of the female are small globular-shaped vesicles containing minute *germ-cells;* these are found in the ovaries of the female in different stages of development. In the healthy female after puberty, one or more of these vesicles become matured, burst and are set free, then make their way through the fallopian tubes into the cavity of the uterus. This maturing and expulsion of an ovum take place every month at each return of the menses. During sexual congress the spermatic fluid is thrown full into the mouth of the womb, here it is transmitted by some mysterious process up through the fallopian tubes to the ovaries, where it unites with the ovum, and conception takes place. Thus conjointly united the male and female principle becomes a new creation, a new human being, which in due process of time develops into an individual which is an exact counterpart of its parents.

Thus it will be seen that certain conditions are necessary if conception is to take place. First, there must be a matured ovum set free from the ovary; this is marked by the menstrual evacuation. Now, abundant observation has shown that conception generally takes place within fourteen days after the entire cessation of the menstrual flow, *very rarely* after seventeen days, and within two days of the commencement of the next period. This leaves four or five days of almost complete exemption from a liability to conceive. There is no period, however, of absolute exemption. Owing to false methods of living, the use of stimulants, and the excitement of the animal passions, the ovum may ripen prematurely and thus increase the liability to conceive.

EVOLUTION OF THE FŒTUS.—After conception the fecundated ovum usually remains quiet within the ovary for about five days. During this time the initial stages of subtle and mysterious vital organization and growth are taking place—processes too mysterious and profound for the successful exploration by the eye of man. "Wonderful arcana of Nature! in which, after all our profoundest scrutiny into the mystery of life, we can discern only the means and the ends, but not the manner. We see the minute representative forms of two lives combined to produce a third, in which shall appear, during all the possible threescore years and ten of its subsequent life, the general characteristics of the nation or tribe to which its progenitors belong; the characteristics of the family as distinguished from those of other families in the vicinity; and, lastly, the personal peculiarities of each of the immediate parents, all of which are impressed upon the embryonic germ, grow with its growth, and strengthen with its strength."—GUERNSEY.

But not only are the striking characteristics of race transmitted, but all observations prove that moral, mental and physical qualities of health and disease are transmitted by both parents, and impressed upon the ovum in the act of impregnation. "The recent developments made in the study of heredity," says Dr. Willard Parker, "show that not only physical but mental and moral qualities are believed to be transmissible. Even instinct is regarded as hereditary knowledge—the offspring inheriting in its physical constitution the acquired knowledge of the parents." If this be so, then, what a fearful responsibility rests upon the parents. Think of the moral depravity, the brutish disposition, the idiocy, the insanity and homicidal tendencies which threaten the extinction of our race, being entailed upon successive generations by the use of alcoholic liquors. Think of the numerous diseases engendered by the use of tobacco, opium, and other narcotics. These are all poisons which are retained in the system, producing nervous exhaustion, and laying the foundation of disease not only in the parents, but in their innocent offspring as well.

People wonder why it is so many children are born into the world with dwarfish forms and feeble constitutions. They marvel at their suffering lives and early decay, but never consider for a moment the important part they act in this great drama of human life,

"But blame heaven for the tangled ends,
And sit, and grieve, and wonder."

If a tithe of the knowledge we possess of what may be transmitted from parent to child be true, then a fearful responsibility rests upon all parents who would preserve the immaculate purity of their offspring, by giving them vigorous, healthy constitutions, free from the taint of disease. To secure these, the first consideration is, they must be *well born*.

PRIMARY CAUSE OF DISEASE.—The parents at the time of begetting must be in all pure and natural and in a healthy condition. The *primary cause* of disease is a hereditary lack of vitality, either in the germ, the sperm, or in the combination of both. And next to this, and proceeding from the same cause, comes the taint of scrofula, consumption, gout, syphilis, insanity, with a long train of other disorders. These are all hereditary, and some of them are manifest in the offspring at an early period of its life. Then, again, there is no doubt that thousands of infant germs are poisoned *in utero* by drug *medication*, while still more are born diseased from the same cause. The mother's blood is poisoned, and from it the infant receives its nourishment.

How sad to contemplate the consequences of parents fastening upon these innocent little ones diseased and enfeebled constitutions, from which they must suffer and perhaps die prematurely, or, if perchance they should live, must drag out a miserable existence the balance of their mortal lives. But Nature is very kind and neglects nothing that can benefit her creatures. She exerts herself at all times to preserve the race, even from these evils; and, with all things working together for good, we must not despair, but try to improve by culture and education, until health and happiness prevail, instead of sickness and suffering and premature death.

FŒTAL DEVELOPMENT.—After conception the ovum remains quiet in the ovary for about five days. During its temporary abode here, important preparations are being made for its reception in the cavity of the womb, where it will reside for the next nine months. The time occupied by the ovum in the ovary after conception and in its passage along the fallopian tubes until it reaches the uterus is from ten to fourteen days. At this stage it is so small that it is with great difficulty it can be found by the closest inspection with a powerful glass. Once in the uterus its growth is rapid, although seven days after its arrival there it is invisible to the naked eye.

By the fourteenth day there is a vesicle formed the size of a pea, and the embryo within it can be seen with the naked eye. Its weight at this period, including the investing membranes, etc., is about one grain.

At twenty-one days it resembles an ant, is about three-eighths of an inch long, and weighs about four grains.

At three months it is about four inches long, and weighs from one and a half to two ounces.

At four and a half months it has increased in all directions; the bones and muscles have become so far developed that the fœtus moves them forcibly, and the prospective mother can usually feel its motions from this time forward. This is called the period of "quickening."

At six months the nails of the fingers and toes may be distinguished. A little fine hair is found upon the head, the whole form of the child is distinct, its usual weight is about two pounds, and its length from ten to twelve inches.

At seven months every part of the fœtus is so far enlarged and so far matured that if born it might live to grow up, if properly cared for. Its weight is from three to four pounds, and its length from twelve to fourteen inches.

From this time up to *nine months,* the usual period of birth, all the organs have acquired that degree of development and solidity requisite for the perfect performance of their respective functions. Its weight is from seven to nine pounds, and length from eighteen to twenty-two inches. There are some cases where the fœtus has been ill-nourished that do not weigh more than two or three pounds; on the other hand, cases are not rare that weigh from twelve to fifteen pounds. The largest infant at birth, of which we have any well-authenticated record, weighed 23¾ lbs.; height, 30 inches; breast measure, 24 inches; round the head, 19 inches; foot, 5½ inches in length. The parents were very large people; the mother was 7 feet 9 inches, and the father 7 feet 7 inches in height.

CHAPTER IV.

PREGNANCY.

The Prospective Mother—Sacred Responsibility—Sexual Indulgence During Gestation—Its Effect Upon the Offspring—Signs of Pregnancy—Cessation of the Menses—Morning Sickness—The Breasts—Quickening—Duration of Pregnancy, etc.

The generative function has for its special object the continuation of the species, and it is intimately connected with the highest order of organic and animal life. The woman who assumes the relation of mother takes upon herself the most sacred obligations of humanity. No period of her life is fraught with greater responsibilities than that of utero-gestation, or the time during which she carries the embryo in her womb. The influence which she exerts upon the future physical and, we may add, moral and intellectual condition of her offspring, during this eventful period, is of the greatest importance. Everything that disorders her system affects the child. If her blood is pure, the child is built up in purity. If she has an abundant vitality, her child drinks from a full fountain. Indeed, there is no condition of the mother, mental or physical, which may not have its influence upon the child and the future welfare of society. No people understood this so well as the ancient Greeks, who surrounded the pregnant female with everything which was calculated to perfect mental and physical development: music, statuary, paintings, works of art, and everything which appealed to the higher senses. Women were taught that among their highest aspirations should be the bearing of perfect children. Therefore, if ever the laws of health are strictly obeyed by the expectant mother, they should be during the period of gestation.

From these considerations comes the law that every woman by her supreme right to herself has the right to decide whether and when she shall have a child. She is to carry it, to bear it, to educate it; she is responsible to her child for its paternity and its development; and this responsibility carries with it the right of choice in all that affects it; and if she would transmit to her offspring a sound and healthy constitution, she is in duty bound to preserve her own health by living in accordance with the physiological laws of her own being. And while the direct physical influence of the father on the child ceases after impregnation, he is nevertheless under the most sacred obligations to love and tenderly care for the would-be mother, and in all things endeavor to promote her happiness. In this way he may not only encourage and strengthen her, but contribute largely in giving to her child a healthy and harmonious development. During the state of pregnancy women are more sensitive, nervous, and excitable; an unkind word or look, any indifference or neglect shown, may produce a deep and lasting impression upon the future well-being of the child. Every husband ought at this time to manifest towards his wife the most thoughtful consideration, the kindest care and the most tender love. Looking at all the facts, then, it must be apparent to every intelligent person what the duty and conduct of parents should be during this eventful period when an immortal being is born into the world.

SEXUAL INTERCOURSE DURING PREGNANCY.—Nature's rule, by instinct, makes it devolve upon the female to determine when the approaches of the male are allowable. And no one acquainted with the wisdom of nature, in all her operations, will doubt that the prohibition of all sexual intercourse among the lower animals during pregnancy must be for a wise and beneficent purpose. It is a law of all nature—

a law that is said never to be violated even among savages, outside of Christendom—that there should be no sexual union during gestation. "There is no male in the universe that abuses his mate in this way but man," and no woman can submit to such abuse without injury to herself and danger to her offspring. Medical writers agree that the predisposition to that terrible disease, epilepsy, in children is caused by the unnatural excitement of the animal passions during pregnancy. In the adult this disease is frequently developed by excessive venery, and the child born with such a predisposition will be exceedingly liable to it in its early years. And it is well known to every physician that it is a frequent cause of miscarriage, chronic inflammation and ulceration of the womb, with a variety of sympathetic nervous disorders that torment and harass the prospective mother. By the nervous exhaustion which it gives rise to, it is believed to effect the mental capacity of the offspring, and even to aid in developing the idiotic condition. We feel assured if parents could be made to realize the injurious effects which the abuse of the animal passions engenders, especially upon the mother and offspring during the period of gestation, they would be willing to restrain their passions and accept that which should commend itself to their reason and judgment, and which is in harmony with the Divine laws of their being.

SIGNS OF PREGNANCY.—The limits of this work will not allow us to go into details on this subject; we must be content with stating a few of the prominent changes which take place when the female becomes pregnant.

CESSATION OF MENSTRUATION.—One of the first circumstances which lead a female to suspect that she is pregnant is the non-appearance of the *menses* at the proper time, and if, at the second period, they are still absent, it is deemed almost conclusive. This is one of most unvarying as well as one of the earliest results of pregnancy.

MORNING SICKNESS.—Most women suffer from nausea and vomiting, especially on rising in the morning; hence it is termed "morning sickness." It may commence immediately after conception, but more generally it sets in about the fifth or sixth week, and ceases soon after the third month, although, in some cases, it continues during the whole period of gestation. This symptom, occurring at the regular time and in the usual manner, is valuable when combined with other symptoms, but when taken alone is more or less doubtful.

THE BREASTS.—About two months after conception the female usually feels an uneasy sensation of fulness, with tingling pains in the breasts and about the nipples. The breasts increase in size and firmness; the areola (circle around the nipples) darkens, and the nipples enlarge and project more than previously. This change is often attended with some pain and tenderness.

QUICKENING.—This term was applied to the mother's perception of the first movements of the fœtus, under the erroneous belief that it was the first movement, as it then became alive or quick. We know now that the fœtus *is alive* from the moment of conception. Quickening, then, or the first motion felt by the mother, usually occurs about four or four and a half months after conception. Moreover, two or three weeks before labor the uterus sinks lower in the abdomen, and the woman becomes smaller around the waist. This is a pretty sure sign of the near approach of labor.

DURATION OF PREGNANCY.—The term or duration of pregnancy is far from being absolutely fixed. It has been known to vary from four to six weeks. There have been cases in which a fœtus of six months has been born, and lived. On the other hand, cases are not unusual in which gestation has been prolonged ten calendar months. Even domestic animals vary weeks in their periods. Hence, the deductions from such cases and from general calculation have led to fixing the term at ten lunar months, or *two hundred and eighty days.*

There are three cardinal points from which, if they occur at the usual time, and in regular succession, a correct " reckoning " may be kept and the time of labor fixed with a good degree of certainty.

First. The time of the last period of menstruation.

Second. The commencement of morning sickness, six weeks after conception.

Third. Quickening, at half-way, one hundred and thirty-five days from quickening to labor.

The usual mode of calculation is from two weeks after the last menstruation; and the time so fixed is corrected by the time at which quickening occurs. In many instances this proves pretty correct; but the uncertainty as to the time of conception, with the variation in the time of quickening, renders the calculation no more than an approximate estimate.

CHAPTER V.

PRESERVATION OF HEALTH DURING PREGNANCY.

HYGIENIC PRECAUTIONS — DIET — OVEREATING — TIGHT LACING — BATHING — VENTILATION — EXERCISE — REST — SLEEP, ETC.

THE pregnant female should observe the greatest simplicity in regard to diet. Her food should be simple, but nutritious; that most consistent with health is composed of farinaceous grains, fresh ripe fruits, and vegetables. Among the wholesome fruits are apples, pears, peaches, plums, grapes, strawberries, blackberries, raspberries, melons, bananas, oranges, nuts, etc.; of vegetables, potatoes, beans, peas, beets, tomatoes, egg-plants, asparagus, cabbage, squash, salad, etc. These furnish abundant aliment of agreeable flavor, sufficient for every reasonable desire. The flesh of animals, if eaten at all, should be indulged in very sparingly. We fully believe that all persons would be better off without the use of animal food, and especially would we advise the woman who has the joys of a mother in prospect to avoid it. The flesh of dead animals is not the kind of food with which to build up the delicate tissues of the unborn infant, nor yet to preserve the health of its mother. Pregnant women who indulge in the use of unwholesome food cannot maintain good health, and such persons cannot supply suitable nourishment for the fœtus *in utero*. False notions in regard to the amount of food required during this eventful period often lead to overeating and consequent derangement of the digestive organs. Little or no extra food is necessary to sustain the simple growth of the fœtus, whose gain in weight is only about half an ounce per day.

As a beverage, pure fresh water and milk are preferable to everything else. All *alcoholic beverages* should be scrupulously avoided. Even tea and coffee are stimulants that cause nervous exhaustion, and it will be better to leave them out of the bill of fare.

BATHING.—Of the importance of personal cleanliness and frequent bathing it is hardly necessary to speak. It has been a necessity of the human race from its creation to the present time; without it man is unfitted for social equality. No amount of personal beauty in features, figure or complexion can compensate for a want of cleanliness. It enhances every charm, and creates new ones peculiar to itself.

In its relation to health, frequent ablutions are of the utmost importance, as must be evident from a knowledge of the structure and functions of the skin. This membrane, "like a seamless mantle," invests the entire body. It is supplied with minute glands which secrete the perspiration. Under ordinary circumstances about two pounds of perspiration are secreted and thrown off by the skin daily, although this amount may be largely increased by exercise, etc. Besides this saline aqueous matter, the skin is continually casting off in minute, powdery scales the old, worn-out cuticle, and this, together with the worn-off particles of clothing, dust, etc., adheres to the surface of the body, mingles with the perspiration and forms a thin, dirty coat on the skin. Now, unless this be daily removed by friction and washing, the "pores" become choked, and the functions of the skin seriously interrupted. Therefore, all who would preserve their health and personal beauty should bathe regularly three or four times a week, and frequently apply the flesh-brush in the meantime.

TIGHT DRESSING.—So much has been said on the subject of dress and tight lacing, that it would seem almost superfluous to speak of it here; and yet nine-tenths of the fashionable ladies at the present time dress in such a manner as to compress important internal organs and seriously interfere with their vital functions. There are still those who believe in the traditional notion that the Creator has made a great mistake in the construction of woman by making her waist entirely too large, and other parts of her body much too small. Hence they have undertaken to improve on His handiwork by reducing the size of the waist to make it conform with their ideas of what constitutes modern female beauty. They effect this by means of whalebones, steel plates and strong bands, arranged in such a manner as to encircle the chest and reduce it to the proper dimensions. They have even taken out patents on their novel devices for this purpose, and, if they could, would no doubt reconstruct and remodel the whole human form to suit their fancy. A good idea of what their ideal figure would be like may be inferred by an inspection of some of the dressed models on exhibition in the windows of some fashionable dressmakers.

Singular perversion of taste! wonderful and all-powerful influence of *fashion!* which can induce so many intelligent beings to suffer torture like savages, for the purpose of distorting their bodies, and bringing them into those artificial shapes which civilized nations denominate *genteel* and *graceful*. If women were the only sufferers from these cruel practices the sin would not be so great; but their posterity participate deeply in the consequences which result from their criminal perversity. If a poodle or pet monkey were put into corsets and stays, and their bodies compressed out of shape, like some of our females, the perpetrator, if discovered, would in all probability be indicted for cruelty to animals; but when the same barbarity is practiced on human beings, it is tolerated because considered *genteel* and *fashionable.*

When will people learn that they cannot violate the natural physiological laws in the slightest degree without having to suffer the penalty? Even compressing the feet with tight shoes or wearing tightly-fitting gloves is a frequent cause of headaches and deformities which are neither ornamental nor convenient. The pregnant female, then, of all others, should dress loosely, without compressing any part of the body. All corsets and belts must be abandoned, and tight lacing, by impeding the circulation and preventing the necessary expansion of the abdomen, may cause incalculable injury to both mother and child. Such methods of dressing often cause miscarriage, uterine displacements, heart diseases, and not infrequently malpositions and often deformity of the fœtus.

AIR AND EXERCISE.—Foremost among the

conditions of health is the breathing of pure fresh air and the taking of suitable exercise. The first of these is of vital importance. A person may go without food for weeks, or remain in a state of inactivity for months, and yet enjoy comparatively good health; but to be deprived of atmospheric air for a single moment endangers the very life of the individual; indeed, it is questionable whether such a person can live after having been totally deprived of air for more than five minutes, as shown in cases of drowning, where all air has been excluded.

There is scarcely a subject in regard to the preservation of health of greater importance than the one under consideration. When we reflect that the *impure* or *venous* blood is changed or purified in the lungs by the action of the air we breathe, it follows, as a matter of great importance, that this element should be perfectly pure. The air is composed of one part oxygen and four parts nitrogen, and a small quantity of carbonic acid. The most essential part of this life-giving element is the oxygen it contains, and any diminution or change in this renders the atmosphere unfit to breathe. Now, the quality and purity of the air are affected by every "breath we take," the quantity of oxygen is diminished, and the carbonic acid increased, while the nitrogen remains about the same. Not all the air taken into the lungs is expelled by that organ; a part of the oxygen is retained in the blood, and carbonic acid given out in its stead. Air that has been once respired contains eight and a half per cent. of carbonic acid; hence, when several persons are crowded into a close room the atmosphere soon becomes so vitiated by an excess of carbonic acid and the excretions from the body as to be utterly unfit for respiration. Such an atmosphere poisons the very fountain of life and sows the seeds of pestilence and disease.

Pure fresh air, then, is absolutely necessary for purifying the blood in the lungs. Every part of the dwelling in which we reside should be supplied with pure fresh air. Especially should the sleeping-room be so ventilated that the air in it will be as pure in the morning as it was when entering in the evening. And if such were the case there would be far less suffering from headaches, dizziness, want of appetite, and a host of nervous diseases that too often arise from sleeping in ill-ventilated apartments. By day and by night, then, at all times and in all places, sleeping and waking, we should have pure air and breathe it plentifully.

EXERCISE.—As all organs of the body depend upon exercise for a healthy development, it follows as a natural sequence that exercise is one of the most important conditions in the preservation of health. Active useful labor, or active exercise of some kind, is indispensable for physical development, health and happiness. The kind of exercise needed is varied employments, varied amusements, attractive industry, pleasant society and the gratification of the natural talents. It should be such as to *interest* the *mind* and keep the body in more or less constant motion. Outdoor exercise and open-air sports are, of all others, beneficial to health, and especially to the pregnant female. But lifting heavy weights, making vigorous exertion, riding upon horseback or in carriages driven rapidly over rough roads, should be carefully avoided. Too severe labor or exercise cannot fail to have an injurious effect upon both mother and child; on the other hand, too great indulgence in ease or a lack of bodily exercise cannot fail to result injuriously.

Persons pursuing a business that necessitates sedentary habits or the use of only a few of their muscles should devote a part of each day to exercising those muscles that are not active during labor. Brain workers require an abundance of exercise, so as to keep up a proper circulation throughout the body and to impart vigor to all the various organs.

The mental faculties also require suitable exercise for their development. All observation and philosophy show that intellectual pursuits are not only compatible with, but actually tend to promote physical health and long life. If we diligently acquire knowledge, and continue to exercise the memory, we will retain the intellectual faculties to old age, when the poor physical body will be tottering on the brink of the grave. The same is true of the affections; if they are exercised in the performance of good, noble, generous acts, they will grow stronger from day to day, and we shall come to realize that we have laid up a treasure far more valuable and enduring than silver or gold.

We would impress it upon the minds of all parents that the more of *health* and *happiness* enjoyed by mothers during the period of gestation, the more, other things being equal, will their children enjoy these precious gifts throughout the whole period of their lives.

REST AND SLEEP.—Rest, and especially the rest of sleep, is indispensable for the preservation of health. The brain and all the organs of the body require rest. It is a necessity of the system and must be periodically indulged in. After twelve or sixteen hours of waking and exercise, a sense of fatigue is experienced which demands repose and reparation of the vital powers. Most persons require from six to eight hours of sleep daily, and this amount cannot be materially diminished without injury to the health. As a general rule, the amount necessary to refresh the system is in proportion to the amount of bodily and mental exertion made by the individual.

During sleep the respiration and pulse are both diminished in frequency, and the temperature of the body is reduced about $1\frac{1}{2}°$ from its normal standard. Hence the propriety of covering the body during a nap in the daytime, even in warm weather. Again, during sleep, the *heart* beats less frequently by from eight to ten strokes per minute; this is when the heart gets its rest: obliged to continue in action all the while, it takes advantage of the situation during repose, and works slower, so as to recuperate its vital powers. Nothing exhausts and prostrates quicker than the loss of sleep; therefore, intense study, late hours, night-watching, mental excitement, and the like, are injurious, and should be avoided as much as possible. The use of tea, coffee and narcotic stimulants is a frequent cause of wakefulness and inability to sleep; hence, persons suffering in this manner should avoid all such things.

CHAPTER VI.

DISEASES INCIDENT TO PREGNANCY.

Morning Sickness—Heartburn—Waterbrash—Headache—Piles—Pruritis Vulva—Incontinence of Urine—Constipation—Varicose Veins—Swelling of the Feet—Pain in the Side.

Although pregnancy is, strictly speaking, a natural physiological process, it borders so closely on the morbid state that it is a difficult matter to draw the boundary line between them. In consequence of the latent diseases which have been handed down to us by our predecessors, and the unnatural and artificial lives we lead, it is often attended with deviations from health which it may be necessary to briefly notice here for the benefit of those who are interested in the subject. Hence, in the present chapter we shall refer to the disorders incident to pregnancy as *altered* and not as *morbid* conditions of the system. And, by the way, we may here remark that women of strictly temperate as well as active habits suffer far less from these organic changes than do those of opposite habits. And it is also interesting to know that all the functional derangements resulting from a state of pregnancy disappear with or after parturition.

NAUSEA AND VOMITING.—Prominent among the organic sympathies excited by the pregnant state are nausea and vomiting, and from the time at which the attacks occur it has been termed "morning sickness." It usually begins about six weeks after conception, and continues with more or less violence for three or four months, when it gradually subsides. In some instances nausea and vomiting commence soon after conception and continue throughout the whole period of gestation. It mostly takes place as soon as the patient rises from bed in the morning, and often continues to harass her for two or three hours. After considerable straining and gagging, a mouthful of tough mucus is thrown up, which is often very sour. Food is rarely ejected, but the patient is annoyed by spitting of saliva, which at times is very profuse, and attended with "heartburn" and "waterbrash." In some cases, however, the irritability is so great that all food is immediately thrown up after being taken, and the patient suffers from a two-fold cause—gastric irritation and want of nutrition.

In the treatment of some rare cases it is sometimes necessary to nourish the patient by *nutrient* injections.

HEARTBURN AND WATERBRASH.—This is another form of gastric derangement from which many women suffer during utero-gestation. It may occur at a very early period, and even be amongst the first symptoms by which the patient will recognize her condition. This form of disturbance is attended with pain and heat in the stomach extending upward, sometimes to the throat, with occasional eructations of very sour or bitter fluid, which is sometimes hot and so acrid as to excoriate the throat and mouth. The fluids evacuated may be of a bilious character, or clear, tasteless and watery —hence the popular name " waterbrash." Eating seems to aggravate all these symptoms.

We need hardly add that a judicious diet should be strictly observed. Lemon juice taken in small quantities will be found beneficial in some cases. Sour or sub-sour apples and other fruits are also efficacious.

HEADACHE.—Next to disturbance of the stomach, headache is probably the most common complaint of pregnant women. Sometimes as early as the second week after conception a strange sensation of fulness or heaviness is felt in the head, attended with dulness and a disinclination to active employment. After stooping there is blindness, with flashes or sparks before the eyes; disposition to fall forward when stooping; headache with feeling of weight on top of the head; palpitation of the heart, and general nervousness. The pain may be dull or acute, commencing over the eyebrow and extending to the entire head, with but few intervals of ease. Sometimes there is a fastidious state of the stomach with variable appetite; the smell of food while cooking often sickens the patient, and articles of diet that used to agree with her are now disgusting. These likes and dislikes often continue through the whole term of gestation.

HEMORRHOIDS OR PILES.—The term hemorrhoids is used to designate a number of small well-defined tumors situated around the verge of the anus. They have been divided into external and internal, according as they are developed without or within the rectum. Again, where there is no discharge from them, they are called "blind piles," and when the contrary is the case "open or bleeding piles." They are a source of great suffering to females during pregnancy, and if not in first are in subsequent cases.

PRURITUS VULVA.—This is a not infrequent accompaniment of pregnancy, and forms one of the most distressing disorders to which a female in this condition is liable. It consists of an incessant and *intolerable itching* of the vulva or private parts. In almost every case of pregnancy there is an increase in the secretions of these parts, and sometimes it is very acrid and causes this irritation. The inner surface of the labia and of adjacent parts is often covered with *aphthæ* similar to the thrush of infants. From the parts affected a vitiated watery discharge takes place, attended with the most intense itching, which greatly distresses the patient.

Frequent ablutions with *hot water* are very beneficial. Bathing the parts with a strong solution of *Borax* is also very useful in allaying the itching. These failing, take *Hyposulphite* of *Soda*, half an ounce; *Camphor Water* eight ounces, mix, and use it as a wash three or four times a day.

INCONTINENCE OF URINE.—This very distressing complaint may occur at any time during pregnancy, though perhaps it is more common during the earlier months. The patient is tormented with a constant desire to pass water, and if this desire is not immediately gratified it is discharged involuntarily. The urine is frequently very acrid and often has a strong odor.

CONSTIPATION.—This is a very common attendant upon pregnancy. The pressure of the gravid uterus on the lower portion of the bowels interferes with their normal action and sometimes causes obstinate and prolonged constipation. Almost all the sympathetic affections of pregnancy are aggravated by this condition; it induces general uneasiness, nervous excitement, loss of appetite, restless nights and erratic pains in the abdomen.

Exercise, a diet composed chiefly of fruits and vegetables, and drinking largely of cold water will generally relieve this difficulty.

VARICOSE VEINS.—This condition of the veins is not often met with in first pregnancy, but if it is, even in a trivial degree, it gradually increases in severity with every succeeding pregnancy.

The enlarged veins are generally superficial and may be confined to one or both limbs. At first they assume a reddish hue, but afterwards a bluish or leaden color, and the larger ones become very much knotted; they get larger when the patient stands on her feet or suffers the limbs to hang down. The swelling diminishes when she has assumed a horizontal position.

This affection is not dangerous, and when moderate is not painful, but, if it continues to increase, the coats of the vessels may give way, and a dangerous hemorrhage follow.

SWELLING OF THE FEET.—During the latter months of gestation some women are troubled with swelling of the lower extremities, increasing towards evening, and occasioning a certain amount of inconvenience. The extent of the swelling varies much; it may be confined to the feet and legs, or it may involve the thighs. In some cases the anasarca is still more general, and we find the upper part of the body, the hands and the face œdematous. The effusion is manifestly the result of pressure upon the veins, impeding the circulation.

PAIN IN THE SIDE.—Women are often troubled in the latter months of pregnancy with pain in the right side. It usually comes on about the sixth month and leaves after the beginning of the eighth month. The pain is of a deep-seated aching character in the right side under the ribs. The patient cannot sit long at a time, and mostly finds relief by lying down. Short women, particularly in their first pregnancies, are most likely to suffer in this way.

Like most of the disorders enumerated in this chapter, and which are developed by a state of pregnancy, this one disappears after parturition.

CHAPTER VII.

ABORTION, MISCARRIAGE, FŒTICIDE.

Threatened Miscarriage—Criminal Abortion—Methods of Procuring—Professional Abortionists—Cause and Cure of the Crime.

By abortion is meant the expulsion of the fœtus or embryo from the womb before it is able to live separately from the mother. This accident may occur at any period of gestation, but is most frequent at the third month. The liability is increased at such times as *correspond* to a *menstrual period*. And when it has once taken place the woman is more liable to miscarry again. If it takes place after the sixth month it is called *premature labor*.

It is always an "untoward event," and may exert the most unfavorable influence upon the constitution of the female, blasting the fairest promise of health, and ofttimes laying the foundation for fatal disease.

Threatened Miscarriage.—The symptoms of threatened miscarriage are: A sense of uneasiness, languor, with aching or pain in the back, followed by bearing-down pains in the pelvic region, with slight discharge of mucus or blood from the vagina. The pains extend around the loins to the abdomen and down the thighs, recurring at regular intervals, and increasing in strength and frequency until the ovum or fœtus is expelled.

The treatment must vary according to the condition of the patient and the cause giving rise to it. In all cases the horizontal position and perfect quietude are indispensable.

Having briefly considered abortion as it occurs incidentally, we come to speak of another phase of the subject that ought to engage the serious attention of every Christian man and woman throughout the broad land. We refer to

CRIMINAL ABORTION, FŒTICIDE.—*Its Cause and Cure.*—The increasing frequency of this practice, for the purpose of getting rid of the product of conception and thus preventing the birth of a living child, exists to an alarming extent in the cities and villages, and even in country places. Few are aware of the extent to which this crime prevails in our country; even physicians are ignorant of a majority of the cases that occur among their patrons, for it is generally the services of some unprincipled "doctor," who has a *private* reputation in this kind of business, that are sought after, instead of the regular family physician. After the crime has been committed the family physician is often called in to take charge of the case, not knowing what was the primary cause of the patients' illness, as they will invariably try to conceal this from their friends. In our professional career we have been called upon to take charge of many such cases, and have spent many anxious hours at the bedside of these victims, and can point to individuals whose whole life thereafter has been one of continual suffering from impaired health, to be attributed to this cause. When the subject of abortion escapes immediate death, some form of womb disease is almost certain to follow sooner or later; the few who do escape may deem themselves especially fortunate. Thousands of women, wives and mothers in the higher walks of life, risk or actually sacrifice their lives every year by this unnatural crime, their most intimate friends being uninformed and unsuspicious as to the real cause of their death.

It seems almost incredible that parents, especially mothers, can so far forget their maternal love and moral responsibility as to risk their own lives in wilfully seeking the destruction of their unborn offspring. We may forgive "the poor, trembling victim of some vile man's lust, who, after having been deserted by a man-monster who can forget his own child and the agony of the betrayed mother, seeks thus to hide her shame and escape a lifetime of disgrace and contempt, which is sure to be heaped upon her even by her own sex, while her betrayer is respected and even beloved by professedly virtuous women;" but how are we to reconcile the thought of married women and mothers who seek the destruction of their unborn children? Yet, in the prevalent unnatural condition of society and the diseased state of men and women, morally and physically, it has become a custom of shocking frequency.

There are those who affect to believe that it is a far less crime to destroy a child in the embryo state than after the period of quickening; that at this stage of development it is feeble, without intellect and incapable of an independent existence; hence, being of so little importance, it is no crime to destroy it. This kind of philosophy would justify the taking of life under almost any circumstances, the killing of delicate or sickly children, or even the aged and infirm. It is closely allied to that savage philosophy which justifies the destruction of feeble infants or old, worn-out fathers and mothers on account of their helpless condition. Such a belief has neither reason nor common sense to commend its approval. It is well known that the fœtus in utero has life, and even moves—though it may not be able to make its movements felt—long before quickening, and that its destruction at any time after conception is fœtal murder, and a violation of the Divine command, which says, "Thou shall not kill."

It is high time the good people of our country fully realized the moral degradation and sinfulness of this crime, which now threatens the very existence of our race. The practice is not confined to the lower classes of society, but is found in every station of life—among the wealthy, the poor, the professed Christians, the educated and the ignorant—who systematically procure the destruction of their embryo offspring. In nearly all cases they are actuated by selfish motives, the love of ease, and the desire to evade the duties and cares of a family.

METHODS OF PROCURING ABORTION.—There are various methods of procuring abortion, and as this is in all cases a violent and unnatural process, it is always attended with danger. Sometimes it is effected by means of potent drugs, the mother often being fatally poisoned in the effort to expel the embryo or fœtus. These drugs are extensively advertised in newspapers, secret circulars, etc. They are paraded before the public as "Female Pills," "Monthly Regulators," etc., etc. Sometimes the advertisements are so adroitly worded under a caution as to convey the precise information needed; for example, the female will be advised not to take the "pills" if she is in the "family way," as they will be sure to "bring on a miscarriage." This is a cunningly devised trick to catch the hungry and thirsty.

But the most common method of accomplishing this desired result is by means of a surgical operation, executed by professional *abortionists*. These so-called "doctors" can be found in all the cities and towns of any size throughout the country, ready at any time to commit a base murder for the paltry sum of from *five* to *twenty* dollars—"blood money." The wily victim, closely veiled, wends her way to the place and is ushered into a private room; here she contracts with a *lewd, wicked* person to kill her little babe for a stipulated sum; after the operation she repairs to a "boarding house," where she is taken care of by an accomplice until "she is all right," or is sent home in a coffin. In the latter event, a certificate is given, signed by the "doctor," stating that Mrs. —— died from "inflammation of the bowels;" whereas she died from *puerperal peritonitis* superinduced by malpractice by this self-same "doctor." In other cases the woman goes direct to her home after the operation, and is treated by the family physician, who seldom finds out what caused the miscarriage.

There are those who would fain make light of this crime by attempting to convince themselves and others that it is a trifling offense, and an affair of their own. Such a mode of reasoning, if it can be called such, is too superficial to warrant a reply. The fœtus in utero is a living human being, and as such is deserving of the same care and protection as if it were *born* and lying by the mother's side. The fact that it is feeble and insignificant does not alter the case. The *newly* born infant is small and helpless compared with a man or a woman, which it would soon become if properly cared for. And low, indeed, must be the husband or wife who will permit the love of pleasure, or of ease, or of selfish gratification, to so gain possession of their moral instinct as to lead them to seek the destruction of their unborn babe.

"Of all the sins," says Dr. Gardiner, "physical and moral, against man and God, I know of none so utterly to be condemned as the very common one of the destruction of the babe while yet in the womb of the mother. So utterly repugnant is it that I can scarcely express the loathing with which I approach the subject! Murder in cold blood, without cause, of an unborn child, one's nearest relative ; in fact, part of one's very being, actually having not only one's blood in its being, but that blood momentarily interchanging ! Good God !—does it seem possible that such depravity can exist in a parent's breast—in a mother's heart?"

It is a crime against humanity which should call forth the condemnation of all generous-hearted and loving Christian people. To the credit of the medical profession, be it said, is due, in a great measure, the present state of public sentiment in regard to this matter. Physicans of all schools have condemned it through the press and from the platform, while a few pulpit orators have proclaimed against it as a most degrading sin. A healthy, happy child is the dearest treasure and the greatest blessing that can come to two loving hearts. It must be a terrible necessity that would make any person, fit to have a child, take means to destroy it.

THE CAUSE AND CURE OF THE CRIME.—And now, my humane brother and sister, what are the cause and cure of this great social evil? To the first question we answer, it is the *abuse of the sexual function.* A woman bears the blame of destroying her infant in embryo, but not a word is said of the necessity for her doing this, being the result of brutish, yea, worse than *brutish, indulgence* on the part of her husband, whose unnatural and depraved sexual demands make it necessary for her, time and again, to commit this crime; and her husband allows her to take the risk of her life and incalculable suffering, bodily and mental, rather than say to himself, " this must not be; I am the principal cause of all this trouble, suffering, sin and crime. I am unworthy the name of husband; I am untrue to the vows I made in marriage to love and protect; I will cease to be the cause of or a participant in this crime, by conforming my sexual demands to nature's requirements, which are for the procreation of offspring, and for that only." Then, where both parties are weak, let the stronger sustain the weaker.

We hear it said that " too few children are being born nowadays." The fact is there are far too many, of the kind they are—not too few. If every married pair reared two or four *well-born, well-ordered* children, the world would be well on its way to the millennium. It is cursed with the number that are simply and wholly the result of *lust* and *unbridled passions* of men and women; and as the stream does not rise higher than its source, it is surging on with ever accumulating violence, the outcome of which is murder, rape, incest and the whole catalogue of crimes we see in our midst. Look on the faces of the hundreds of children we meet in the schoolrooms—everywhere. Are joy, love and peace seen on their countenances? No ; but the reflections of unwilling maternity, of willing murder, of sorrows too deep to be written on any other tablet than the human face and soul, are displayed there for those whose eyes have been opened and whose souls are awakened to the cause as well as to the effect of these horrors the tithe of which has not been computed, much less told. How unevenly, too, the burden of sin and suffering is divided between the guilty pair who willingly risk everything for the momentary gratification of a passion which only love and desire for children redeems from lust.

If the sexual nature was fairly understood and rightly used there would be fewer ill-assorted marriages, to say nothing of those who were right at the start, but became completely demoralized and debauched by over-indulgence; each becoming unloving, diseased, unhappy, disappointed in everything which had been intended to make married life the holy thing it should be, simply by allowing the animal desires to subordinate everything else—self-respect, conscience and even the strongest element of the living organism—self-preservation. If there is anything to be pitied in this world it is the subject of repeated unwilling maternities; no man can conceive the depths of desperation and mental and physical wretchedness that follow in their train. It is so hopeless, so unending; only death, and that is not a desirable alternative, ends the great responsibility of this burden (for burden it must be called when unwillingly borne) in this life; eternity only can answer for the future. When we consider that it requires great courage or great cowardice on the part of man to deliberately take his own life—a thing we believe is rarely done in a perfectly sane condition—we may estimate the desperation or courage or madness that overcomes a woman's fear of death when she essays to destroy a part of her being, risking the whole. Good, conscientious women, who would not have been capable of destroying the smallest creeping thing before this unnatural state of things was brought about, find themselves in a state of wretchedness to which death is preferable instead of their elysian dreams of wedded love; they yielded their scruples till they were no more, the vice once horrid to them became a thing to be desired, an alternative to welcome. With repeated sins, and an ever ready accomplice—the one nearest to her in relationship and worldly interest—her judgment becomes so impaired that she loses all sense of moral obligation; the sin not being in the act of committing abortion so much as in the sinful life of indulgence which has led to the result.

And now, what is the remedy for this evil? There is one that is natural, simple and effectual, as we have already intimated; now we will state briefly and distinctly what it is: STOP THE PRODUCING CAUSE. The man and and woman who do not wish to have children must keep apart. This is the only safe and right way to avoid unwilling maternity. We can see no reason why any one should be compelled to bear children who wishes to avoid them. Two young persons who have flirted and danced together, and passed through a fashionable courtship, then stood up before a priest, in white kid gloves and satin, surrounded by evergreens and orange blossoms, and vowed eternal love and fidelity to each other, have no right to regard such a pledge as a license for *sexual indulgence*. So long as there is *licensed lust* in marriage there will be *criminal* abortion; we can never cultivate the moral sense in woman while she is degraded in this highest element of her being. "The Divine law of continence is not annulled by any usage or enactment of human framing; and no formula pronounced by magistrate or clergy, no mutual covenant between partners in a sin, avails to make uncleanness holy." In righteousness and innocence will the remedy for all humanity's ills be found, and if we will cease to do evil and learn to do well, then will the conflict be all the more easily won; but do not make the mistake so many thousands have done in opening the battle when it is too late.

CHAPTER VIII.

LABOR—PARTURITION.

PRELIMINARY PREPARATIONS—MAKING THE BED—POSITION FOR DELIVERY—PREMONITORY SYMPTOMS—CHARACTER OF THE PAINS—THE AFTER-BIRTH.

It is not intended to give a minute description of the process or management of labor on this occasion, as no one but a qualified physician would have the temerity to take charge of such a case, unless placed under very peculiar circumstances. A few suggestions to govern the nurse or attendant until the arrival of the physician are, therefore, all that will be aimed at here.

The woman who has the joys of a mother in prospect will see that everything necessary for the occasion is at hand, so that all confusion may be avoided when that interesting period arrives. The room she is to occupy should be in readiness, and, where there can be a choice, it should be large and airy, on the sunny side of the house, and as retired as possible. In winter the temperature should be about 65° F. during labor, and 70° afterwards.

To Prepare the Bed.—When labor has fairly commenced, the bed should be prepared, which is done by placing a square of oil-cloth or a gum-blanket over the mattress at that part of the bed which will be occupied by the patient's hips; over this the under sheet is spread, and upon these, two or three sheets folded square, on which the patient is to lie. After the labor is over, these folded sheets should be removed, but the oil-cloth is allowed to remain. If the patient's bowels have not been freely evacuated within twelve hours of the onset of labor, they should be freed by a thorough injection.

Position for Delivery.—If now the pains are forcing and labor advancing, the patient should undress and go to bed. The position for delivery is on the left side, the hips being close to the edge of the bed, and the knees drawn up towards the abdomen. The night-dress should be tucked up underneath her, beyond the hips, to prevent soiling; a pillow placed between the knees; and she may be allowed to grasp the hand of an attendant.

This is the most natural position for the patient to assume during labor; and, while it is not necessary to remain in the one position all the time, when the infant's head is low down and distending the soft parts, she should make no material change until after labor is completed.

LABOR, or parturition, completes the grand function of reproduction; and, as stated in a previous chapter, it takes place about *two hundred and seventy days* after conception. It is a natural physiological process, and among the savage tribes it is attended with very little pain or sickness; but in civilized society, where the people are out of correspondence with the Divine order, it is often protracted, and attended with a great amount of suffering.

PREMONITORY SYMPTOMS.—There are a few premonitory symptoms which indicate the approach of labor, such as nervous trembling, depression of spirits, looseness of the bowels, frequent inclination to pass urine, and a slight discharge of reddish mucus from the vagina. The pains generally commence in the lower part of the abdomen, and are then felt in the back, extending gradually to the front. They recur at *regular* intervals, and increase in force and frequency.

During the early stage they are of a "cutting or grinding" character, causing an outcry on the part of the patient. But as labor advances they change to "bearing-down or forcing" pains, which compel the patient to suspend her breath and suppress the outcry. From this time forward the pains become more frequent; they succeed each other so quickly that a new one commences before the former has quite terminated. At length the force conquers all resistance, and the head is expelled; after this there is a short interval of rest, when the uterine power is again exerted to expel the body of the child.

This part of the labor being accomplished, a sense of great relief follows, to the inexpressible joy of the mother.

DELIVERY OF THE AFTER-BIRTH.—An interval of half an hour, more or less, now elapses before the uterus again contracts to expel the after-birth, and by one or two pains its connection is severed with the uterus, and the labor is completed. Sometimes, however, the after-birth does not come away for several hours, unless removed by some one competent to do so; it is a delicate operation, and should not be undertaken by any one not skilled in the art.

CHAPTER IX.
HOW TO CARE FOR THE BABY.

A Dependent Creature—The Nurse; Qualifications of; Duties of—Reception of the Infant at Birth—Cutting the Cord—How to Wash the Baby—How to Dress the Navel—How to Dress the Baby—The Diaper—Care of the Mother—State of the Bowels—The Lochia—Vaginal Injections—Duration of Confinements.

A NEW-BORN infant is said to be the most dependent creature in all the world; naked, helpless and unable to procure food for the sustenance of life, at the same time it is the most wonderful and complex piece of machinery in all of God's creation. Endowed with faculties yet in an undeveloped state, they are capable of wonderful achievements if properly cultivated. How important that we understand its needs, and how to take care of it; how to wash it and how to dress it, and how to feed it, and how to nurse it, and how to educate it, and how to give it that moral and intellectual training that will fit it for the important duties and responsibilities of life. It is the bud that should be cared for if the flower is to arrive at maturity.

It is the seedling that must be properly cultivated and protected if it is to grow to be a healthy vigorous plant. And the same is true of man; unless the infant is tenderly cared for and nourished and taught the lessons of life, it can never attain that perfect physical and mental development of which it is capable. Therefore, no inexperienced mother or simpleton of a nurse is competent to look after the physical, mental and moral prosperity of a baby; mothers especially should know all about the caretaking and management of children, and not be at the mercy of ignorant nurses. And at this point of our inquiry it would seem necessary to say a few words on the qualifications of

The Nurse.—One of the first qualifications of a nurse is good *common sense*, to begin with. No ignorant or superstitious person is fit or should be allowed to have the care and training of a baby. It is one of the most important duties that can engage the attention of any thinking mind, and yet one that has been more neglected than almost any other. Until recently the care of a child was haphazard; any ignorant old woman was supposed to be fully competent to take charge of a baby, and "bring it up in the way it should go;" but, fortunately for the rising generation, people are beginning to realize the importance of having intelligent and qualified persons to care for their children and nurse others when they are sick.

In addition to being intelligent and well trained, a nurse should be *healthy;* be free from all eruptive diseases, sores, ulcers, etc., and clear of all vices or pernicious habits. She ought to be gentle, patient, firm and cleanly, and whatever she has to do for a patient should be done with great gentleness. It is the *little things*, and the manner of doing them, that count in nursing as in everything else. Adjusting the clothing, changing the bed-linen, bathing the patient, administering food and medicine and performing a thousand other duties, when done with skillful, willing hands, add greatly to the patient's comfort and prospects of recovery.

Persons when sick are often very irritable and restless; taken suddenly from an active life and confined to bed, perhaps racked with pain, they become very impatient, and require great consideration and forbearance on the part of the nurse. Sometimes it is necessary for the nurse to be very firm; but it must be remembered that firmness is not rudeness. We cannot expect a suffering patient to know as well what is best for him or her as those who are well with clear heads. Therefore, if it is best to do a certain thing, do it, but do it kindly.

Cleanliness is said to be next to godliness, and a nurse should keep the sick-room clean and neat. *A constant supply of pure atmospheric air is an absolute necessity in the sick-room.* And everything that has a tendency in any way whatever to corrupt or vitiate the atmosphere of the room should be removed. All perfumery, as cologne, musk, scent-bags, camphor, smelling-bottles, and quack nostrums, should be excluded, and nothing but the pure fresh air of heaven allowed as respiratory food. The absurd notion of keeping the room close and warm, under the apprehension of the patient taking cold, is a fruitful source of ill-health, and tends to foster disease and prevent recovery. If a current of air passing through the room is so dangerous to the occupant as some people seem to believe, is it not strange we do not all die instanter when exposed to the open air or a sudden gale of wind? The truth is, people suffer from what they call "taking cold" by breathing *bad air*, and not from too much good air. The reason coughs and colds are more prevalent in winter than in summer is because the people live in close, ill-ventilated rooms, breathing foul air, which poisons their life-blood, causing chills, fever, headache, pain in the bones, and inflammation of the mucous membrane of the air-passages; these they denominate "a cold;" whereas in summer the houses are thrown open, and the pure fresh air of heaven is allowed to flow in from all quarters, and hence we seldom hear of colds during that season. It should be borne in mind that bad air will poison the system as surely as bad food.

Again, all offensive odors, the dressings from wounds, soiled clothing and the like, should be promptly removed from the room. All vessels should be emptied as soon as used and carefully washed. Remember, a very little thing will spoil the appetite of a person already sick. Never allow food to remain in the room if the patient cannot eat it, and do not let *drinking water* or *milk* stand long without being changed, as they absorb all gases that may be in the room; for if the patient drinks these he will be taking back into his system the poisons which have been thrown off through the skin and other organs of the body.

In the preparation and administration of food, great skill and adroitness are required on the part of the nurse. The physician in attendance is expected to name the articles of diet for the patient, and the nurse is supposed to know just how to cook and to serve them.

When the patient has "a poor appetite" and is very fastidious, the better plan will be not to consult her about what she would like to eat, but surprise her with a new regimen, done up in good style. Spread the tray with a snow-white cloth, put on the best china dishes, have the silver shining brightly, and the food nicely adjusted, then take it promptly to the patient; this will often have a salutary effect in stimulating the appetite. Remember, the mind exercises a wonderful influence over the appetite, as is often witnessed by the effect of bad news and other mental emotions on persons in the enjoyment of health.

Having briefly spoken of nurses and nursing, we again take up the previous subject of

RECEPTION OF THE INFANT AT BIRTH.—It frequently happens that the child is born before the arrival of the physician, and in such an event it is well to know what should be done and how to do it.

After the head is born there is generally an interval of rest before the pain expels the body; while in this position the head should be supported by the hand of the nurse, and if the cord be coiled around the neck, it should be disengaged or drawn down, so as to prevent strangulation. When the child is born, place it a little out of the discharges, and *expose its face to the open air;* if the mouth or nostrils are obstructed by mucus, remove it with a soft napkin. If the child be healthy, and not injured in the birth, it will cry lustily as soon as it is born, and its skin will change from a light leaden hue to a pink or rose color.

CUTTING THE CORD.—As soon as respiration is fully established in the child, and *pulsations have ceased in the cord*, the child may be separated from the mother. To do this, take a piece of small twine or other string, put it *once* around the cord, about two and a half inches from the abdomen, and tie it firmly in a hard knot; cut off the loose ends, and tie another string one inch further up; then, with a pair of scissors, sever the cord between the ligatures. Having done this, wrap the child in a warm blanket, or something similar, until ready to be washed and dressed.

HOW TO WASH THE BABY.—As soon after the child is separated from the mother as convenient, it should be carefully washed; to do this, take a little hog's lard or sweet oil, and rub it thoroughly over the entire body, and especially in the arm-pits, groins, between the buttocks, and wherever the limbs are folded upon each other; then take a piece of *dry flannel,* and wipe the child until it is clean and dry. This will remove the white unctuous matter that usually covers the skin of new-born infants, and which adheres to the parts with great tenacity. After this a little warm water and fine soap may be used to remove the grease. The eyes and mouth should be washed with clear water, care being taken that no soap enters the eyes. It is important to have the child perfectly clean at this first bathing; by observing care in this respect, scaly eruptions and excoriations of the skin will in many instances be avoided.

The *temperature* of the room should be moderately warm, and the child bathed at least *once a day;* at first, the water used should be about new milk warm, but the temperature should be gradually lowered, and after a few weeks may be used cold. Never bathe a child in a *cold* room, but have the temperature a little *warmer* than the water to be used. During the daily process of bathing the infant, its mind should be amused and its attention attracted in such a manner as to make the operation one of pleasure instead of pain. Even at this tender age the little creature may be taught to be patient and even happy under trying circumstances. It should be borne in mind that every act of the mother or nurse towards the little infant is productive of good or evil upon its character as well as health.

Even the act of washing or dressing may be made to discipline and improve or aggravate its temper, and thus exert an influence upon its whole future life. The parent and nurse therefore, should always treat the infant as a sensitive and intelligent creature from the very first hour of its existence.

How to Dress the Baby.—In the dressing of a new-born infant the first thing to be attended to is the umbilical cord, or that portion of it which remains attached to the abdomen. It has long been the practice among physicians and nurses to wrap around the cord a strip of muslin or old linen, after the fashion of wrapping up a sore finger. It is then laid up towards the child's breast, and a compress, made of several thicknesses of soft muslin or linen, placed over it, and the whole kept in place by a flannel bandage, five or six inches wide, placed around the child's body and secured by three or four pins. This is the usual method of dressing the navel. The cord generally comes off in five or six days, but the bandage is kept on in many cases until the child goes into short clothes. This time-honored custom of bandaging the infant is open to serious objections: in the first place, nine times out of ten it is put on *too tight*, producing unequal pressure upon the abdominal walls, and not infrequently causing rupture. It is a source of irritation and discomfort to the child, and interferes with the functions of digestion.

How to Dress the Navel.—Take a small pad of absorbent cotton, say six inches long and three inches wide, make a hole in the center, pass the cord through this, laying the pad lengthways with the child's body; now lay the cord up towards the child's breast and fold the lower end of the pad over it, and secure the whole by a light flannel band, merely to hold the dressing in place until the cord comes off, when the band should be discarded, there being no further use for it.

How to Dress the Baby.—It is scarcely necessary to describe the usual method of dressing the baby; every expectant mother or nurse is familiar with the little linen shirt, with saw-teeth edging around the neck; the long flannel petticoat, with wide inelastic band at the top; the dress, and lastly the diaper. The garments thus made and put on in the usual way are not only uncomfortable, unphysiological, but absolutely injurious. A moment's thought will convince any sensible person that an inelastic band placed around an infant's chest, reaching from the armpits to the navel, and pinned tightly—over two fingers is the old rule—must necessarily interfere with the free expansion of the lungs during the first weeks and months of an infant's life. We must remember, the walls of the chest are easily compressed and deformed at this early period of life. Another objection to this form of garment is, the chest is warmly clad while the shoulders are left with only a slight covering—the dress. Again, the skirt is folded from side to side over each limb, and the bottom turned up and pinned, so that the little one cannot kick and use its limbs as it will want to do.

There is a better way to dress the baby, infinitely better, in "The Gertrude Baby Suit." This suit is the design of Dr. Grosvenor, of Chicago, and is constructed as follows: The undergarment should be made of nice fleecy goods—Canton flannel is the best we have at present—cut princess, reaching from the neck to ten inches (twenty-five inches long) below the feet, with *sleeves* to the wrists, and having all the seams smooth, and the hems at the neck, wrist and bottom upon the outside—the latter turned over once and felled or cat-stitched with colored worsted—a tie and one button behind. Here you have a complete fleece-lined garment, comfortable and healthy, and one that can be washed without shrinking. The next garment is made of baby flannel (woolen), also cut princess, same pattern, only one-half inch larger, reaching from the neck, and may be embroidered at pleasure. The dress cut princess to match the other garments is preferable.

The ordinary baby *dresses* are all right, except that I would have them only from thirty inches to a yard in length.

Now, these three garments are put together *before* dressing, sleeve within sleeve, and they are put over the little one's head at once, and buttoned behind, and the baby is dressed, there being but *one* pin—a diaper pin—in baby's dress instead of *fifteen*. No shoulder blanket should be used, because it is sometimes over the head, sometimes about the shoulders and neck, and sometimes off entirely, and these changes are exposures. Accustom the little one from the first to go without it.

At night the dress should be simply a Canton flannel night-dress and a diaper—the dress being not unlike the undergarment in the suit, only a little longer. It is absurd to think that a child can rest sweetly in a diaper, a bandage, a petticoat pinned tightly around the chest, and a double gown, as many a child is expected to do. A good rule is to "dress the little ones as you would love to be dressed if you were a babe." There is nothing wonderful about this simple dress. The only wonder is that we have dressed our little ones so *badly* so long.

THE DIAPER.—The diapers should be made in two pieces, the outer one cut triangular-shaped, of one thickness, the long edge being selvaged to avoid the hem. The other piece, made, say, ten inches square, is folded in the form of an envelope and placed in the center of the outer piece when being applied, and the diaper put on in the usual way and fastened with a safety-pin.

This form of diaper saves the heat and discomfort of so many thicknesses over the hips and kidneys, and has the advantage of a small piece to wash for the soil and plenty of sop where most needed. The cotton flannel is softer, warmer and more absorbent than linen or any other material. The hem is turned once on the right side and run through the machine. Use fleecy side next to the baby.

The main advantages of this method of dressing the baby are:

1. Perfect freedom to all thoracic, abdominal and pelvic organs.

2. That all the clothing shall hang from the shoulders.

3. The greatest saving of the time and strength of the mother in caring for the babe, there being but one pin instead of fifteen.

4. The resulting health and comfort of the child.

5. The evenness of the covering of the body, there being the same covering over the shoulders as elsewhere.

Owing to the extreme sensibility of infants to atmospheric changes, and for other reasons, we believe wool-flannel should be worn next the skin, at least during the winter season. The clothing should be *warm and light*, and its protective quality should be uniform for the whole body, except the head, which is suitably provided for by nature. The flannel should be of *fine soft wool*, to avoid undue irritation, and to keep the skin moist and healthy. Such flannel seldom, if ever, produces rash or discomfort of any kind; if, however, it should be found to irritate the skin in rare cases, or in very warm weather, a slip made of thin silk or linen may be put on under the flannel as a protection.

THE DRESS SHOULD BE LOOSE.—The garments should be made to fit *loosely*, so as not to impede the circulation, compress the parts, or restrain the motions of the body or limbs in any manner. Babies are generally dressed *too tightly;* their bones are as elastic as cartilage, and their flesh is soft and yielding, so that the slightest constriction of the parts may so interfere with their natural development as to cause suffering and deformity that may continue for a lifetime. Hence the necessity of dressing the child as loosely as possible, so as to give the utmost freedom to all parts of the body while it is in this undeveloped state. Remember that *children need exercise, even in early infancy;* they want to kick and perform a thousand other muscular movements, which they will not be able to do if hampered by tight or heavy clothing, and when it is improperly put on. Again, they are frequently wrapped in blankets or shawls and held closely in the arms of nurses, when they become restless and fretful, because prevented from moving their limbs and bodies about, agreeable to the impulses of their own nature. The fact is, children are nursed and carried and "fussed with" entirely too much; it would be far better to give them a place on a bed or lounge, with full liberty to exercise their muscles and amuse themselves. During the first three months of its existence the infant should be handled but little, and never placed in an erect or sitting position; nor should it be jolted, or tossed up and down—a practice nurses frequently indulge in—as the bones are soft and pliable and the joints are imperfectly developed; hence there is danger of injury to these delicate structures, causing disease and often deformity.

Let the infant, then, be warmly clad, its

clothing principally of flannel, and so distributed as to cover all parts of the body alike, neither tight enough to impede the circulation nor obstruct the breathing, nor long enough to prevent its kicking and the free use of all its limbs. Its arms and neck should be covered as well as the legs, and the diaper should be loose, so as not to chafe, and fastened with a *safety-pin* to guard against accident.

CARE OF THE MOTHER.—After delivery the patient should be made as comfortable as possible, that she may rest and sleep, if need be. When fairly rested, the child may be put to the breast and allowed to nurse until it is satisfied. There may be no milk in the breasts as yet, but a watery secretion will be found there adapted to the child's wants until the "milk comes." The child should be applied to each breast alternately in order to prevent overdistension in either, and to guard against the formation of abscesses. Should the breasts become lumpy and painful, bathe them gently with *hot lard*, and keep them well drawn.

STATE OF THE BOWELS.—It is perfectly natural for the bowels to remain in a torpid or inactive condition several days after delivery. In a majority of cases they will be moved by the end of the fifth or sixth day. Should any discomfort arise in consequence of constipation, an injection of lukewarm water may be administered and the bowels relieved. *In no case should purgative medicine be given during confinement.* Any woman who takes a dose of *purgative medicine* soon after delivery endangers her life, and while many escape who do take oil and other laxatives at such times, they run a fearful risk by so doing. We have known cases where a single dose of cathartic medicine taken soon after childbirth caused inflammation of the womb, followed by intense suffering and death in a few hours. Many such cases occur, and the friends never suspect the cause. The infant is often made sick and to suffer from colic, griping pains and diarrhœa, from nursing the mother after she has taken such drugs. So strong is the prejudice on the part of some mothers and nurses in favor of giving cathartics at such times, that the nurse will often give a "dose of oil" or some other purgative without even consulting the attending physician.

OF THE LOCHIA.—The discharges from the vagina, which take place after delivery, are called *lochia.* After the first few days, until about the tenth day, these discharges are similar in appearance and quantity to the menstrual discharges. In a majority of cases the red color leaves about the tenth day, and it is usually succeeded in its turn by a whitish or mucous discharge.

VAGINAL INJECTIONS.—The importance of cleanliness during confinement cannot be overestimated. The vagina should be syringed daily by the nurse with lukewarm water. If the lochia be dark in color or offensive, a solution of *Carbolic Acid* should be used. To a pint of *tepid* water add a teaspoonful of the acid, and use this as an injection. This will keep the parts clean and guard against fever from blood poisoning.

DURATION OF CONFINEMENT.—For the first three or four days after delivery the woman should remain quiet in bed, keep her mind free from excitement, and live on plain food, such as light puddings, farina, cornstarch, oatmeal mush, toast and similar articles, and, as a drink, water, chocolate or milk. If now all goes well she may rise daily to have her bed made up, and gradually return to her ordinary diet. The first week should be chiefly spent in bed, or at least in a recumbent position, during which time all visitors should be excluded from the room. A woman ought not to leave her room, or go up or down-stairs for two weeks after the birth of the child.

CHAPTER X.

HOW TO SAVE THE BABY.

Beautiful Structure of—Chances to Live—Mortality of—Statistics—Teething Sickness—Cause of Death among Infants—Faulty Alimentation—Constipation—Taking Cold—Overfeeding—Three Meals a Day—Deficient Lactation—Prescribing Stimulants, etc.

The several subjects already discussed bring us to the consideration of the one of paramount importance—the baby—one of the most complex and beautiful structures ever turned out of the workshop of Him who doeth all things well. "Imagine to yourselves," says Dean Close, " that lovely and beautiful object, a naked newborn babe; gaze upon it. Is there anything more beautiful, or more curious, in creation than that little infant? See its structure. Is it not curiously and wonderfully made? Look at its little hands; see how it plays with its little fingers, as if it wanted to touch; how it stretches its little feet, as if it wanted to stand; how its eyes look into vacancy, as if it wondered at the new world into which it had been brought. All its faculties, indeed, are in the lowest state of development, but there is a promise of wonderful results. Look at it again as the handiwork of God. Take each of its organs of sense. Look at its eye; go and consult the oculist, and he will explain its wonderful structure; there is the mirror upon which external objects are to be reflected; there is the protection afforded by the eyelid and eyelash; and there is the marvelous adjustment of all the parts for the purpose intended. Look, again, at the ear, at once a drum and a trumpet formed for the conveyance of sound. Look at its lips, its tongue, and, by and by, at its teeth, and ask the elocutionist how marvelously this combination of organs results in the divine faculty of speech. There is the body of the future man; look at it and see the handiwork of God."

Such is a graphic description of the new-born infant "so fearfully and wonderfully made." The mother has suffered in her travail, and the husband has grieved over his wife's sufferings, while sympathizing friends have waited at her bedside; and now the innocent babe that sleeps by her side is the happy reward for the sickness and pain she had to endure. At first, helpless to a degree, it invites her sympathy and protection; as the stream of life gains power new feelings of love expand her maternal heart. Soon the infant by a smile rewards the fond mother, and by its little exclamations of pleasure makes her rejoice with exceeding gladness. Day by day it grows more interesting, giving evidence by its childish prattle of opening intelligence, and soon it becomes a "wellspring of pleasure," and is endeared to the hearts of all who come within its influence.

But how different the picture when disease overtakes it! How grief-stricken and dejected the mother! How sad and how sorrowful the father, while all the household within are distressed by its pitiful moan. The little creature itself, how changed; behold how haggard its face and how emaciated its form. The mother, in her devotion, still waits upon it with unceasing love; self is forgotten in her anxiety, while she watches over it through long dreary days and nights. But who can tell how soon, like the tiny floweret or tender blossom, it may wither and die.

INFANT MORTALITY.—It is said that a new-born babe has a less chance to live a week than a man of *ninety*, and less chance of living one year than an *octogenarian*. The records of mortality prove that nearly *one-third* of the infants born, die before they reach the end of the first year, and that ten per cent. more succumb before reaching two years. In the cities of Philadelphia and Baltimore nearly fifty out of every one hundred children die before reaching their fifth birthday; and in New York City *fifty-three* per cent. of the total number of deaths occur under the age of five years. During the months of June, July and August, 1887, 4119 children under the age of one year died in this city alone. We could give the figures to corroborate this statement, were it necessary; but as few persons have a desire for the dry details of statistics, we refrain from giving them here.

In England and France the ratio of deaths among infants is very similar to that of our own country. In Yorkshire, England, *one-fourth* of them die before they are a year old; and in Leicester the death-rate is still greater, more than four infants in ten being swept off in the first few months of their existence. In France the case is more terrible. At Paris *one half* die ere they reach *four* years. This is a fearful cost at which the battle of life is fought and won. It is absolutely shocking! And this mortality is not confined to the wretched poor nor to the crowded tenement houses in densely populated districts, but is found everywhere, among the rich as among the lowly, among the educated and the illiterate.

Now, is this mortality a necessary evil? We say not, and believe it arises in a great measure from *preventable* causes. "It certainly," says Dr. Dawson, "cannot be supposed that the Creator intended that all these little ones should suffer and die. There is every proof to the contrary. Has He not wisely and beneficently adapted all their physical wants to the circumstances in which they are supposed to be naturally placed? Has He not surrounded them with every condition and requirement necessary for the maintenance of life and health? For the very preservation of life has He not ordained certain laws to be observed, the neglect of which necessarily brings disease and premature death?"

How, then, are we to account for this terrible mortality? Nearly all writers who have endeavored to explain it assign bad ventilation, improper food, dentition, want of cleanliness, etc., as the principal causes. The first of these—defective ventilation—will, no doubt, lessen the chances of life, but will hardly account for the increased death-rate which occurs in the summer season, when all, the rich as well as the poor, have their houses and windows thrown open and well ventilated. Want of breast-milk is one of the several causes, and a powerful one, no doubt; still it must be obvious, from the number of infants that die who receive their mother's milk, that its injurious effects are exaggerated, and the great majority of deaths are evidently due to some other cause.

TEETHING SICKNESS.—The process of dentition or teething is believed by many to be a potent factor in causing the diseases and mortality among infants. It always seemed strange to us why the human infant should be subjected to so much sickness and suffering while getting its teeth, which is a natural physiological process. All the other organs of the body are perfected without any unusual disturbance, and the young of the lower animals "cut their teeth" without any manifestation of pain or discomfort whatever, so far as can be observed. Why the Creator should inflict all this punishment on the infant alone during the process of teething is beyond our comprehension. We do not believe that He does. The truth is, we are all "living out of the natural order." "In no sense," says Dr. C. E. Page, "is sickness an incident of teething." And Dr. B. F. Dawson, Physician to the New York Dispensary for Sick Children, declares: "If there ever was an absurd fallacy fastened upon the popular mind it is, in my opinion, this bugbear of 'teething sickness.'" And these views are supported by many other leading physicians and scientists who have devoted a large share of attention to the subject.

CAUSE OF DEATH AMONG INFANTS.—In pursuing this inquiry, we find that the great number of children that die under one year of age— over 75 per cent.—is due to *gastro-intestinal* disorders. Dr. Ballard published in the British and Foreign Medico-Chirurgical Review, for 1870, an article on "Infant Mortality," in which he shows that during a period of five consecutive years there were in England 314,-242 deaths of infants under one year of age, and of this number, 277,852 were due to diseases of the *digestive organs*—over 88 per cent. Dr. C. E. Buckingham, of Boston, states that in 1870 there were 9,873 children who died in Massachusetts under five years of age, more than one-half of whom died from intestinal diseases. Dr. B. Dawson says: "Of 11,381 children under twelve years of age, treated at the Dispensary for Sick Children, in New York City, during three years, 3,243 were suffering from diseases of the digestive organs." And this seems to be true of whatever town or country from which the report is selected.

FAULTY ALIMENTATION.—What then is the inference to be drawn from this great preponderance of gastro-intestinal disturbance and terrible mortality from the same among infants? Do not the facts in the case point to an unhealthy or defective system of dietary? It is our belief, verified by experience, that it is the immediate or subsequent result of *faulty alimentation,* chiefly through the prevailing ignorance as to the proper requirements of the infant's stomach, and especially to *excessive feeding—too many meals and too much food at a time.* Everything goes to prove that the food received into the stomach must be taken in such quantities and at such intervals as will admit of its perfect digestion and assimilation. Unless these conditions are faithfully observed disease of the digestive organs in some form is almost sure to follow sooner or later. The stomach of a healthy infant is capable of digesting and assimilating a certain amount of food daily, sufficient for the child's normal growth; if this amount be exceeded the surplus will not be digested and appropriated by the system, but will be expelled by frequent purging, puking, increased urination, etc., the methods of nature to get rid of the excess.

The same law in regard to eating applies to grown persons. Dr. R. C. Fisher, of Washington, D. C., says: "It seems to be a more and more acknowledged fact in the ordinary experience of life that 'we eat too much,' and my own experiments for eighteen years with regard to the relation of food to the needs of the organism have taught me that no one is in danger of starvation who eats a pound of vegetable food a day and nothing more. The liability to every form of disease is incalculably decreased for the moderate eater, and proportionately increased for the man who constantly overtaxes his digestive organs."

CONSTIPATION OF INFANTS.—Constipation of infants is another and common trouble, the result of excessive and too frequent feeding. "The explanation of this," says Dr. B. F. Dawson, "is quite simple. The stomach being overburdened with food, and consequently overtaxed with work, each supply of milk, instead of being coagulated into fine and soft coagula, which are readily acted upon by the secreted pepsin, comes into contact with the semi-digested coagula of the preceding meal, and, in consequence, is coagulated more rapidly than it should be normally, the coagula being larger and harder. Such masses, if not ejected, pass into the intestinal canal, but little if any changed by the digestive process, will impact together, and from their size and dryness are with difficulty passed along the bowels, thus giving rise to constipation, colic, etc." Overtaxing the digestive organs by eating too often and too much deranges every function of the body. If the food is not taken up by the absorbents and used by the system in the formation of new tissue, and in repairing the waste which is continually going on in the body, it rapidly undergoes chemical *decomposition* in the alimentary canal, causing flatulence, colicky pains and other symptoms of indigestion.

TAKING COLD.—Again, the excretory organs become deranged from the same source, which often leads to the retention of waste matter in the system, clogging the circulation and producing a species of *blood poisoning*, characterized by lassitude, fever, watery eyes and mucous discharge from the air-passages; these symptoms are usually denominated a "cold," but are nothing more nor less than a *surfeit fever*. We think it safe to say that not one in twenty of the so-called colds is due to exposure or sudden changes in the weather, as generally believed, but to derangement of the digestive organs from the use of improper food or overindulgence in eating.

It cannot be too firmly impressed upon the minds of parents and nurses that it is not the *quantity* of food swallowed by the infant that *nourishes* it, but the amount it can *digest* and *assimilate* that insures the happiest results; but this simple truth is one which, in practice, is constantly lost sight of. It is a custom almost universal to stuff the infant with something almost as soon as it is born, and the practice is kept up at night as well as by day, feeding it every two or three hours, and even oftener, for with some mothers and nurses every cry means *hunger*, and must be quieted with additional food. This is particularly the case during the first year of the infant's life, and hence the greatest mortality is at that period. After this age they are fed less frequently, and we have fewer deaths in consequence.

OVERFEEDING THE BABY.—If there is any logical or physiological reason why an infant should be fed more frequently than a grown person, we would be glad to know it. The saying that a "growing child" requires more food accordingly than a grown person is unsupported by either reason or analogy. Any farmer who has had experience in stock-raising can easily demonstrate the absurdity of such a proposition, for it is well known that a calf will gain steadily in flesh and add *sixty per cent.* to its weight in six weeks on *two meals a day*—fed on cow's milk at that. The " old mother cat " seems to understand the philosophy of digestion and assimilation better than some human mothers or " experienced nurses," for she will leave her kittens—sometimes for five or six hours—and when she returns, instead of finding them starved, finds them "alive and akickin." The common rabbit, *Lepus cuniculus*, will leave her little ones from early morn till late at night, when she returns to give them a "good square meal." Think of a young rabbit with its "little stomach" going without anything to eat for *twelve* or *fourteen* hours, and living to grow fat.

THREE MEALS A DAY.—It has been our happy privilege to induce many mothers to adopt Nature's method of feeding the babies, by giving them only *three meals a day*, instead of so many, and the result shows that it has been eminently successful. We could cite many cases that have come under our immediate observation, of babies that have been reared on *three meals a day*, where they gained steadily in weight, remained healthy and happy, sleeping well, and passing through the whole period of *dentition* without sickness or suffering of any kind. These babies were not troubled with colic, diarrhœa, throwing up, or incontinence of urine, as children generally are who are fed on the old traditional plan. There need be no fear of the infant starving. An adult can labor for twelve consecutive hours daily, using his brain and muscles continually, on *three meals* a day, while the newborn infant, who has nothing to do but to "laugh and grow fat," must be fed, according to the traditional notions of our ancient grandmothers, *ten* or *twelve* times every twenty-four hours. The absurdity of the practice is so self-evident that we feel like apologizing to the reader for simply making the statement.

Again, if an infant be fed every two hours during the day, and two or three times at night—and many are fed even oftener than this—it will have taken, say, ten meals in the twenty-four hours. Now, suppose the child is six months old, and weighs fifteen pounds, it will take four ounces of milk at each meal; this would amount to forty ounces a day; but in order not to overestimate the quantity taken, let us call it thirty-two ounces, or one quart, which it would receive daily. Now, suppose the mother is twenty-five years old, and weighs 140 pounds, and her diet cow's milk; she would have to swallow—in order to take as much accordingly as the infant—*ten quarts* of milk every day. Does any sane person believe she could take this amount of food daily and not suffer from *indigestion* or something still worse? Would she be likely to reach her twenty-sixth birthday under a system of *cramming* like this? or would she be not more likely to fall a victim to a "mysterious dispensation of Divine Providence," who persistently refuses to stultify His own laws and produce good results from wrong doing?

DEFICIENT LACTATION.— Again, frequent nursing of the infant by the mother is a common cause of deficient lactation. We have seen many healthy mothers who, on first beginning to nurse, had an abundance of milk, but in a few weeks the secretion would be so greatly diminished that they were compelled to "dry up the breasts"—as they call it—and to cease suckling altogether. These, in most every instance were, in our opinion, the result of too frequent nursing of the infant, exhausting the lactiferous organ and arresting the proper secretion of milk. There can be no doubt whatever that this constant drain upon the mother, by overtaxing the breast and so abusing its power, leads to a cessation of its functions. A deficiency of milk is often the result of exhaustion, or a run-down condition of the system; in other instances it is caused by indigestion and defective assimilation. Amative indulgence also diminishes the quantity of the milk and injures the quality, and where this indulgence excites menstruation and results in pregnancy there is a double misfortune. The child at the breast and the child in the womb are both defrauded. The milk from a well-behaved cow is better for a child than that from a mother who indulges in such a propensity.

The practice of some nurses, and even some doctors, of prescribing porter, ale, beer and other preparations of alcohol for nursing mothers, under the impression that it is beneficial in promoting the secretion of milk, is a grievous error which cannot be too severely condemned. Infants are often kept in a state of intoxication for weeks by the mothers using these beverages. Let no one be induced by friend or physician to drink these beverages, thinking it will increase the flow of milk or give strength—*it will do neither*. It is feeding the babe on poison, and if, unfortunately, the child has any hereditary tendency towards a love of strong drink, this course is actually fostering the tendency. Would it be at all strange if a child raised in this way should grow up with an appetite for alcoholic liquors?

Again, it is well known to every farmer who has had experience in stock-raising that to allow a calf to run with its mother, and suck whenever its inclinations dictate, will very soon "ruin the cow as a milker;" hence, for prudential reasons, the wise farmer only permits the calf to indulge in two meals a day.

So, then, considering the subject from whatever standpoint we may, we find the frequent feeding or stuffing of infants is attended with serious consequences, and should be abandoned; it is irrational, unphilosophical, and has neither reason nor common sense to commend it to favor.

CHAPTER XI.

HOW TO FEED THE BABY.

The old Method—Feeding and Dosing—Importance of Starting Right—Three Meals a Day—Baby's First Meal—Dyspepsia of Infants, etc.

This is one of the most important subjects that can engage the attention of any mother or nurse who may have the care or management of an infant. Before entering directly upon its consideration, however, we wish to say a few words on the method of feeding the baby as inaugurated by our ancient grandmothers, and which has been handed down to us by tradition, and is generally adopted by parents and nurses even at the present time.

When we reflect that nearly all the diseases to which the infant is liable in the early periods of life may be fairly traced to faulty alimentation, the importance of the subject at once becomes apparent.

Feeding and Dosing.—The custom of feeding an infant on sweetened water, gruel, panada and other slop victuals, soon after it is born, is not only wrong, but absolutely injurious.

No sooner is the child washed and dressed and made comfortable than the nurse, with cup and spoon, is on hand to "feed the baby" "to keep it from starving," under the silly impression that it must be very hungry after its nine months' imprisonment in the little "house not made with hands." And here the *trouble begins*. Having taken its first meal—usually of sweetened water or gruel—the child soon becomes uneasy, frets and cries with pain caused by the improper food it has taken, which is undergoing fermentation in the stomach. Not being able to make known its wants by words— having no language but a cry, by which to plead for the righting of its wrongs—it screams in a most pitiful manner to the discomfort of the tender-hearted mother and all others around. The "good old nurse," with her boasted "experience," still believes it a "hungry cry," issues her second order for rations, and this time gives it cow's milk and water well sweetened; the effect of this will be to aggravate rather than relieve the little unfortunate victim. Recourse is now had to "catmint tea," "calamus tea," "soot tea," "paregoric," "soothing syrup," or some other nostrum, by means of which another form of gastric irritation is added to the already existing disturbance. Thus, between the two—stuffing and

HOW TO FEED THE BABY. 127

drugging—the very life of the helpless infant is put in jeopardy, and, if it escapes the doom of death, is left to drag out a miserable existance the rest of its days. Thousands of these little ones suffer from almost constant narcotism, begun and fostered in this way by ignorant parents and nurses, and are either poisoned out of the world ere they have seen the end of the first year, or they grow up sickly, with depraved appetites and weakened intellects, to fall victims to the vice of intemperance. It is our honest conviction, founded upon extensive observation, that the abuse of the digestive organs in early childhood, by frequent and overfeeding, the use of condiments, tea, coffee, and quack nostrums vended under the bewitching names of "Soothing Syrup," "Infant's Cordial," "Nerve Tonic," "Golden Bitters," "Blood Purifier," etc., leads in after years to the development of the drunkard's appetite, and the misery of the drunkard's career. How can we expect an infant, dosed with anodyne mixtures and narcotic stimulants during the first two or three years of its life, to grow to manhood and not have a morbid craving for strong drink or its twin sister, *tobacco ?*

The digestive organs of the new-born infant being thus prostrated and enfeebled, all the painful consequences of indigestion are sure to follow in its wake; such as acidity, flatulency, colic, vomiting, diarrhœa, green and griping stools, emaciation, and a long train of other disorders. Nine-tenths of these distressing ailments which afflict the infant in the first half year of its life are the result of indigestion, caused by stuffing and dosing the child soon after it is born. If its tender stomach be filled with sweetened water or gruel a few times during the first two days of its life, the chances are ten to one that it will be unable to digest the mother's milk when she is able to supply it.

The fact that in nearly all cases the mother is unable to furnish milk for the baby until it is at least two days old shows the impropriety of giving it artificial food, and the necessity of waiting until the "milk comes." Nature can always be trusted with the management of her own affairs, and as she has been successful in the production and development of a lovely human being, "created a little lower than the angels," she may safely be trusted to manage its diet, and will in nowise leave it to suffer and starve.

It may seem like a trifling matter to put into the stomach of a new-born babe a few spoonfuls of sweetened water or catmint tea (by the way, we know one of these "experienced nurses" to give an infant a *pint of cat-*

mint tea before it was twelve hours old, and she declared to us that it "*cried all night with the colic,*" notwithstanding her efforts to relieve it), but it is doubtful if it ever entirely recovers from the effects of such an attack made upon it in the "house of its friends." Whenever anything is taken into the stomach, either in the form of food or drink, which is not readily digested and assimilated, it is sure to produce more or less gastric derangement; there is scarcely any part of the organism which is not called into morbid sympathetic action by such a condition. Here, in the central organs of life—the digestive organs—is found the starting point, or place of beginning, of a large majority of all the diseases that occur in childhood. And there is every reason to believe that the gastro-intestinal disorders known as indigestion or dyspepsia, from which so many people suffer, are the result of overfeeding and drugging in early infancy.

IMPORTANCE OF STARTING RIGHT.—How important, then, it is to start right in this matter, to avoid all errors and excesses in feeding the new-born infant, whose tender stomach is so easily deranged by improper food and overfeeding, and which is the cause of nearly all the gastro-intestinal disorders with which the infant has to suffer. We must rely upon nature to furnish the infant with proper food for its sustenance, and which is in harmony with its healthy growth and development, namely, the mother's milk; it should have no other food but this until after dentition, unless the mother be diseased in some way to make her milk unsuitable, or in case of her death, when it could not be obtained; in such an event a wet-nurse should be procured, or cow's milk, suitably prepared, furnished as a substitute.

Do not stuff the new-born infant, then, with artificial food, but wait for coming events; it does not require food of any kind, except that furnished by the mother, which will be forthcoming in due time; if fed otherwise the infant will be sure to suffer from flatulence, sickness and pain; and the chances are that when the "milk comes," and the mother is prepared to supply the child's wants, it will refuse to nurse and in all probability be unable to digest the milk when it is taken. No fears need be entertained if the breasts do not secrete milk for forty-eight hours or even longer, the baby will not starve. Nature can manage these things far better than parents or "experienced nurses," or even the doctors; the great danger to strive against is *feeding too often and feeding too much.*

THREE MEALS A DAY.—The question, then,

How often to feed the Baby, is of the greatest importance; and at the threshold of the inquiry we would impress upon the minds of all parents and nurses the necessity of *starting right* in this matter; remember, "a good beginning is half the battle," and generally determines whether the conflict for life shall be won or lost.

As previously stated, the mother seldom has milk for her babe until it is two or three days old; nevertheless it should be put to the breast a few hours after birth, as it not only teaches it to suck, but invites an early flow of milk. There is a watery or whey-like secretion found in the mother's breast before the child is born or at the time of its birth, which is a wise provision of Nature to supply the wants of the infant as soon as it enters the world. This early secretion, called *colostrum*, is the *first food* that should enter the infant's stomach; no sweetened water or artificial food of any kind should be given for reasons already pointed out. If the mother is healthy, her milk is undoubtedly the most natural food for the child; nor should it be fed on anything else until it gets its first or temporary teeth.

Baby's First Meal.—After the child has been washed and dressed, and the mother fairly rested, the infant should be put to the breast and receive its *first* meal. It should be allowed to nurse until its wants are satisfied, when it may be removed from the mother, placed in a comfortable position and permitted to sleep as long as it will. After the first meal it should be nursed *regularly* three times a day, say at 6 A.M., at 12 M., and at 6 P.M., but *never during the night.* This may seem to the mother or nurse—who has been accustomed to feeding a baby every two hours during the day, and two or three times at night—like a "starvation diet," but if *they* could be induced to take food as often, and as much accordingly, as the infant, they would possibly change their minds in regard to this matter. Indeed, the thought fairly considered ought to convince any intelligent person of the impropriety of this frequent and excessive feeding. No one will contend for a moment that an infant can thrive unless it is properly fed, but this by no means implies that it must be stuffed a dozen times every twenty-four hours. *Three meals a day* will be found ample to satisfy all demands of the infant and insure a healthy, vigorous growth of the system; feeding it oftener than this is not only superfluous, but absolutely injurious. If, however, it is found after a fair trial that the infant does not thrive or gain in weight as it should do, a fourth meal may be tried. A healthy child will gain in weight from four to six ounces per week, and if this ratio be maintained right along, no fears need be entertained for its welfare. But if little or no gain is made, the food is either not suited to the child's wants, or the child itself is not right, and needs the care of a judicious physician. The fact of an infant fussing and hunting around as if after something to eat is by no means a proof that it needs food; it is often thirsty and wants water, which should be given to it frequently. There is every reason to believe, as we have endeavored to show in a previous article, that the cause of the many gastric disorders among infants, and which sweep so many of them out of existence every year, is due almost solely to excessive and too *frequent* feeding. The infant's stomach—like the adult's—requires *seasons of rest*, and if this law is violated, disease will surely follow. Many an infant is restless, fretful, unable to sleep, in a word, made sick by this continual stuffing on the part of mother or nurse, notwithstanding it springs from the kindest promptings of the human heart. But we are told that the infant "frets and worries," and can only be quieted by giving it something to eat. The *overfed* baby always has a morbid appetite, and will seldom refuse food so long as it can swallow; like the adult dyspeptic it experiences temporary relief by the ingestion of food, and hence it becomes restful for a time, only to suffer the greater in the end.

DYSPEPSIA OF INFANTS.—It is sad, indeed, to think of the new-born infant—perhaps not a week old—suffering from that fearful malady, dyspepsia. And sadder still is it to realize that parents are responsible to a very great extent for this sickness and suffering to which these helpless infants are liable. For we have every reason to believe that it is the result of too frequent and excessive feeding, which it is in the power of parents to control. And since it has been abundantly proved that an infant can be well nourished on *three meals a day* with the happiest results, no argument is needed to show that more is necessary. And as the *cramming* system has been long and thoroughly tried, with what results it is unnecessary to repeat, we would appeal to every true-hearted mother to try the "new departure," and, our word for it, you will never have cause to regret it. Begin as soon as the baby is born—with the *first meal—start right*—for if you wait until bad habits are formed, you may have some trouble in establishing your rightful prerogative. Remember, the infant begins to take in the situation of things with the first breath of life, and that an unwise or indiscreet nurse may, in a very short time, teach a child habits that may prove not only troublesome, but very exacting.

CHAPTER XII.

HAND-FEEDING OF BABIES.

DIVERSIFIED VIEWS — PROFFERED ADVICE — IGNORANCE ON THE SUBJECT—VARIETY OF FOODS—SUBSTITUTES FOR MOTHER'S MILK—COW'S MILK, HOW TO PREPARE —WHEATEN GRUEL—HOW TO GIVE THE BABY FOOD —POSITION WHEN TAKING FOOD—HOW TO WEAN THE BABY—DENTITION—CLEANLINESS—VENTILATION —TOBACCO SMOKE, POISONOUS EFFECTS OF.

THE mother's milk, as already stated, is the natural food for the infant, but, unfortunately, it often happens that she is unable to furnish breast-milk for her child. Many infants have to be fed artificially from the first, as their mothers are utterly unable to suckle them at all. Where disease of the parent exists, such as scrofula, consumption, cancer, insanity, syphilis, and other dangerous hereditary complaints, the infant ought not to derive its nourishment from this source of contamination, and hence a substitute must be found.

There is perhaps no question upon which the profession as well as mothers and nurses are more at variance than the character of the food to be given in place of breast-milk. Not long since there appeared in a Philadelphia newspaper an article signed "A Young Mother," asking what she should do to save her baby; being obliged to feed it by hand it could not retain or digest milk or cream. The editor offered a prize of ten dollars to any one giving the best answer. This appeal brought out over a hundred responses from mothers, nurses, grandmothers, doctors, druggists and others. Some advised pure milk from one cow; some took it from two cows, and others from a herd; some advised skimmed milk; others the same diluted with water; some one-third water, some two-thirds; others cream and water; others milk with cornstarch, barley water, oatmeal, arrowroot, lime water, brandy, cognac, port wine and lager beer; others recommend Mellen's food, prepared granum, condensed milk, Valentine's meat-juice, Scotch oats essence, and others goat's milk and whisky. One writer says: "Condensed milk, lime water and Grove's anodyne are great for babies, and if they do not thrive on these they won't thrive on anything;" others, to relieve the little sufferers and to "keep peace in the family," advise fennel-seed tea, catnip tea, peppermint tea, whisky and covering the stomach with spice plasters. Some of the therapeutic philosophers advised a little asafœtida, bicarbonate of soda, saccharated pepsin, lactic acid, subnitrate of bismuth, oxalate of cerium, chlorodyne, paregoric and good whisky when certain gastric disturbances arise.

Here, then, we have a specimen of the unanimity and wisdom displayed in the feeding and rearing of infants in the year of our Lord one thousand eight hundred and eighty-nine. There is one notable feature in all this proffered advice from mothers, nurses and doctors, and that is the unanimous agreement, with two or three exceptions, that the baby should be. *stuffed* " every two hours ;" one mother says it should be " fed every two hours, day and night." Another says, "Give plenty of milk. I give my babies a quart of the best milk every day for two months, and then two quarts thereafter, besides rice water and two teaspoonfuls of Husband's magnesia every other day." The *magnesia*, no doubt, is a necessity to purge off and help get rid of the *surplus* or *excess* of milk.

With such treatment is it at all strange that *one-third* of the babies die before they are a year old? The strange part to us is that *two-thirds* do not die instead of only one-third. But babies are very tenacious of life, and will " pull through " sometimes under the most unfavorable circumstances, as if preordained to be the " survival of the fittest."

A Substitute for Mother's Milk.—When the mother's milk is out of the question we know of no better substitute than cow's milk, which will be found to agree more generally with the infant than any other article of food. But there are several points to be considered in the selection of cow's milk. It will be better to take the milk from the product of *several* cows rather than that from one, as it is likely to be more uniform in character. For a new-born infant the cows should be fresh, or nearly so, and they should be carefully fed and cared for. Cow's milk is slightly *alkaline*, but sometimes when the cow has been milking several months, it becomes acid. To test this, take a narrow strip of *blue* litmus paper and dip one end into the milk; if in a short time the paper turns *red* the milk is acid and unfit for a *young* child. Good milk will turn *red* litmus paper blue.

To Prepare Cow's Milk.—For many years we advised pure fresh milk from one cow, diluted *one-third* water, for a three months' babe, but of later years we have used the preparation suggested by Prof. S. P. Sharpless, who is high authority on this subject, and we find it eminently successful. "The best way to prepare cow's milk for a young child," says Prof. Sharpless, "is to allow the milk to stand a few hours until a portion of the cream has raised; then carefully remove the cream. At each meal take the proper potion, place the vessel containing it in a dish of hot water for a sufficient time to warm it, sweeten slightly with *sugar of milk*—never with cane sugar, as this is almost certain to *sour* the stomach. No definite rule can be laid down for the amount of food necessary for the million; but it will not vary much from a *pint* for an infant of *six months*. This amount, divided into *three* meals and given at *regular intervals*, say at 6 A.M., 12 M. and 6 P.M., will be found to give the best results. Never feed the child *during the night*, for that is the time set apart for *rest* for all the organs in the body. As the child grows older the quantity of milk may be gradually increased, so that at the end of twelve months it should take about a *pint and a half daily*. Never refuse an infant *water*, but give even the youngest a few teaspoonfuls frequently between meals. Babies often wish the breast or bottle because they are *thirsty* and not hungry."

WHEAT GRUEL.—If cow's milk cannot be had that *suits* the child, then we must look for a substitute, and in the long list that is presented we know of none that is so likely to suit in all cases as gruel made from *fresh, unbolted wheat flour.* Take a small cupful, stir it in a quart of cold water, and boil gently for *three-quarters* of an hour (use a water-bath or farina-kettle, otherwise it will require constant stirring), when it will be reduced to a pint; strain this through a closely woven cloth to take out all the *coarse* parts, sweeten slightly with *sugar of milk,* and add a pinch of salt. If too thick to pass through a nursing-tube (if that be used) dilute with a little warm water, or, in some cases, with a few teaspoonfuls of *fresh* milk. We have known many babies raised on this preparation of food who had every appearance of being at death's door, and could not retain or digest cow's milk of any kind. We can recommend this diet, notwithstanding all that is said against the use of *farinaceous* food for young babies.

How to give the Baby Food.—A hand-fed baby should receive its food out of a *glass* or *china cup* from a teaspoon. The objections urged against this method of feeding babies are of little consequence in comparison with the advantages which it has over "bottle-feeding." It is less trouble, less expense, and far better for the babies. There is not the same temptation to feed the child so often when the food is given in this way, while the trouble of cleaning and taking care of nursing-tubes, gum nipples and "baby-bottles" is avoided.

POSITION OF THE CHILD WHEN TAKING FOOD.—A child should not receive its nourishment while lying down, but should be supported upon the arm or lap of the person feeding it, in an easy *semi-erect* position, which is the *natural* one; it is pleasanter for the child, there is less risk of strangulation, and besides there is an anatomical reason for this. The practice of dandling or jolting infants soon after taking food is very improper and should not be indulged in.

HOW TO WEAN THE BABY.—In discussing the conditions to be observed in weaning the baby, we would lay down the following rules as essential to the preservation of the child's health and that of the mother:

1. Under ordinary circumstances the child shall have cut at least *eight* of its teeth before the attempt is made to wean it.

2. The child should not be weaned until it has become accustomed to taking other kinds of nourishment.

3. After the process of weaning is decided upon, it is better to execute it gradually. The practice of suddenly taking the child from the breast is not only cruel, but is attended with danger to both mother and child. Cow's milk will be found the best substitute for the mother's milk. We would commence the

weaning by giving the child mother's milk for breakfast, cow's milk for dinner, and mother's milk for supper; this method should be continued for several days; then give cow's milk for breakfast and dinner, and mother's milk for supper; continue this for five or six days, and then withhold the breakfast milk altogether.

4. Teach the child to receive the milk out of a cup or glass, and not out of a nursing-bottle.

5. A child ought not to be weaned while it is suffering much from the irritation of teething or any acute disease, unless there are considerations on the part of the mother which render it necessary.

6. As a general rule, the child should be weaned when it is about *eighteen* months old.

DENTITION.—The eruption of the *first teeth* is very irregular; it takes place approximately in the following order: The two *middle lower* front teeth make their appearance generally when the child is about six months old. In three or four weeks afterwards the *middle incisors above* come through; then the two *lateral* incisors below, followed by the two above. In about two months after these the *first molars* (jaw teeth) are cut—two below and two above. After another respite of about two months the two *stomach* and two *eye* teeth show themselves, and finally, at the age of about two years, the four back jaw teeth—two above and two below—make their appearance; this completes the first dentition, consisting of *twenty* teeth.

It will be observed that the process of teething is accomplished in groups; and the child should not be weaned during the eruption of one of these groups. And, where it can be done, the *cooler* months should be preferred for making this change of dietary.

HYGIENIC PRECAUTIONS; CLEANLINESS, VENTILATION, ETC.—Much has been said and written in regard to keeping all nursing-tubes and food-vessels clean and sweet, the importance of personal cleanliness, and the breathing of pure atmospheric air; these all are necessary for the preservation of health and the enjoyment of human happiness. Breathing *impure air* will poison the system as surely as eating *impure* food; one is just as detrimental to health as the other.

TOBACCO SMOKE.—No one can breathe the foul odors generated by filth, or an atmosphere polluted by *tobacco smoke,* and not suffer to a greater or less extent. All the diseases of infancy are aggravated or rendered more malignant by the habitual breathing of impure air. There is overwhelming evidence to prove that infants especially—who are more susceptible to all impressions than grown persons—are often seriously injured by breathing an atmosphere contaminated with *tobacco* smoke. Not long since we were consulted by a young mother in regard to her baby, which was then eighteen months old. From birth it had been healthy and bright until within a few months, and now it was pale, emaciated, languid, had a poor appetite, was fretful, restless, and had a slight cough. The father was a mechanic and was seldom at home except during the night. We could not understand the child's illness and our failure to cure it. At a subsequent visit we observed that the air in the room where the child was, smelt strongly of tobacco smoke. The father had been out of work for two or three months and at home most of the time. He was in the habit of frequently smoking in the room where the child stayed. The odor of tobacco in the room at once suggested to our mind the cause of the child's sickness, and we said to the mother: Mr. S. must not smoke in the house any more where baby is, "for we believe it is suffering from the poisonous effects of tobacco." Just then Mr. S., who had stepped out, came in, and Mrs. S. read the "riot act" to him, then gave the house a good airing, which had a most salutary effect upon the child, as it soon began to improve, and was not long, as a consequence, in regaining its wonted condition of health.

In a recent number of "The People's Health Journal" Dr. Thos. G. Roberts, in an article on "The Use of Tobacco," mentions the case of a little girl who came under his professional care, which puzzled him for several weeks before he was enabled to find out what was the cause of the child's illness. She "had a poor appetite, was nervous and constantly ailing, though at no time seriously sick." After a time he learned that a "relative of the child often smoked in the house where the little patient lived." He finally concluded that tobacco was the cause of the illness, and had her removed to a place where no tobacco was used, and she "promptly and permanently recovered her health." Dr. Roberts cites a case taken from the "Pall Mall Gazette." The story is told by the mother, and we give the essential points in her own words: "I have one child not yet two years old, a fair-haired, blue-eyed pet, who was as healthy as the birds when she was born." "For a year past she has ailed mysteriously." "I could not say she was ill, yet she was never well." She had no appetite, constantly complained of sickness and disordered digestion. "I took her away by myself to a country town for two months. After the first week she flourished like a young bay-tree; ate and drank and laughed and played, and I was kept forever enlarging her garments. One week after our return home all the old symptoms returned; loss of appetite, dark lines under the eyes, restless days and sleepless nights. I was about to take her away again when she caught a severe cold and was confined to one room for three weeks. She recovered her general health completely while shut in the nursery; appetite, spirits, sleep, all returned. She joined us downstairs again, as usual, and in less than a week sickness and all the old symptoms returned. For nearly three months I racked my brain to find out the cause of this trouble. Suddenly my husband was summoned into the country. A week after he went the child began to eat with a relish, and in a fortnight she was her own happy self, full of notions and spirits. 'Her father never saw her like this,' I remarked one evening when she was so merry and glad, and then the truth flashed upon me: it was his tobacco that upset her. He has been away a month, and the child has gained in flesh and is the merriest, healthiest little mortal possible. He always smoked after breakfast and after lunch, with her in the room, neither of us dreaming that it was injurious to her. But for his providential absence this time, I doubt if it ever would have occurred to me, and we might have lost our darling, for she was wasting sadly. This is a true, unvarnished statement, which my nurse can corroborate."

There is no doubt that thousands of little ones are annually slaughtered in the homes of their friends by this *narcotic poison*. The smoker or chewer is so filled with its effluvia that he can be detected by it the moment he enters the room. All who come near him suffer in their senses and in their health to a greater or less extent. Many delicate infants, and grown persons as well, are poisoned even to death by the smoke and odor of tobacco used by persons around them. Recently we visited a young man who was suffering from a pulmonary affection; he was lying on a couch in a small room and was coughing almost continuously; his father sat near by smoking his pipe, while the room was literally full of the fumes of tobacco smoke. Coming in out of the pure, fresh air of heaven, we felt as if we could not live in such an atmosphere, and immediately threw open the windows. Mr. B. said he was "afraid Johnnie would take cold." We told him we were "afraid he would suffocate," as the air in the room was not fit for a human being to breathe.

It is wonderful what an amount of ignorance and stupidity is shown in regard to this matter by persons ordinarily intelligent, and we can only account for it from the well-known fact that the use of this narcotic poison stupefies and imbrutes those who are under its influence.

CHAPTER XIII.

THE EARLY EDUCATION OF CHILDREN.

OBJECTS OF EDUCATION—TEACH OBEDIENCE—PUTTING CHILDREN TO BED—THE BOOK OF NATURE—EVIL ASSOCIATIONS—SEXUAL KNOWLEDGE—WHERE DID THE BABY COME FROM—EVIL EFFECTS OF ALCOHOL—THE TOBACCO HABIT—THE OPIUM BONDAGE.

THE moment the child is born and opens his eyes to this world his education begins, and it is at this early period of his existence that he should be taught the true lessons of life. "Train up a child in the way he should go, and when he is old he will not depart from it," was the saying of a wise man; hence the importance of starting aright in this primary school where the first lessons of life are taught, which are of such vital importance to the present and eternal welfare of the individual.

OBJECTS OF EDUCATION.—The principal objects of education are: to teach a child useful knowledge, to eradicate his evil propensities, to bring out his noble qualities, to make him a useful citizen and a worthy member of society, and last, though not least, a Christian not only in name, but in reality. A child's intellect is educated or developed by being taught truths by others, and by his learning or storing the memory with various kinds of knowledge derived from the senses. His training and teaching are always going on; everything he sees, hears or does is a part of his education and enters largely into the formation of his character. The most important duty which parents have to perform in this world is to train and properly educate their children; and society has no higher duty to perform, and none more important, so far as the welfare and preservation of our race is concerned, than to look after and care for the rising generation.

TEACH OBEDIENCE.—Among the first lessons taught a child should be that of *obedience.* "Children, obey your parents," is a command of great significance, not only as affecting their safety and health, but also their moral character as well. It is the first yielding of unrestrained will to rightful authority, and as such has an immense significance. The child should be required to do his parents' bidding, and never to feel that he can disobey them in the smallest degree. Gentleness and firmness should characterize all the words and actions of the parent while giving commands which it is expected the child will obey. By pursuing a determined course in this respect, obedience will become a pleasure to the child instead of a burden, and he will come to love and respect his parents, which he can never do if allowed to disobey and follow his own inclinations.

PUTTING CHILDREN TO BED.—"Not with a reproof for any of that day's sins of omission or commission. Take any other time but bedtime for that. If you ever heard a little creature sighing or sobbing in its sleep, you could never do this. Seal their closing eyelids with a kiss and a blessing. The time will come, all too soon, when they will lay their heads upon their pillows lacking both. Let them, then, at least, have this sweet memory of happy childhood, of which no future sorrow or trouble can rob them. Give them their *rosy youth*. Nor need this involve wild license. The judicious parent will not so mistake my meaning. If you have ever met the man or the woman whose eyes have suddenly filled when a little child has crept trustingly to its mother's breast, you may have seen one in whose child's home 'Dignity' and 'Severity' stood where 'Love' and 'Pity' should have been. Too much indulgence has ruined thousands of children, too much love not one."—FANNIE FERN.

Bribing Children.—Parents should never bribe the child in order to make him obey, but require him to yield obedience as a *duty* and because it is *right*. This is the only solid basis upon which to build a moral, upright character. Neither should he be coaxed nor promised rewards nor threatened with punishment to induce him to do right; all such incentives are selfish and tend to belittle and lower the true standard of character. But, on the contrary, begin at the earliest possible moment, even before the child is born, to instil into his life a *love of right*, purity and virtue; then will he go forth armed with the shield of righteousness, safe from the assaults of passion and vice, so long as he adheres to noble principles.

The Book of Nature the Child's Primer. —The perceptive faculties of the infant are brought into requisition at a very early period of life, and he is a very active if not an accurate observer of things. By taking advantage of his observing and inquisitive disposition to direct his attention to natural and familiar objects, a vast .amount of useful knowledge may be communicated to him at an early age without endangering his mental faculties. The mother should be his principal teacher, and the canopy of heaven the main roof over his school-room; most of his lessons should be taught out in the open air, while the fresh breezes are blowing and God's blessed sunshine is beaming upon him. The Book of Nature should be his primer; and the green fields and trees, and mosses, and beautiful flowers—the violets, and daisies, and buttercups, and forget-me-nots, and wild roses—these, together with an infinite variety of birds, robins, and thrushes, and bobolinks, and orioles, blackbirds, and the little wrens, and a thousand others; their habits, their customs, their histories and dwelling-places—all furnish material for his instruction more profitable than any school-books at his early age can do; and such instruction, imparted by the mother's loving voice and affectionate manner, will make a deeper and more lasting impression upon him than anything he may learn from the books of man. Little boys and girls who are taught these useful lessons from Nature while they are young, and while their hearts are tender, will not be likely when they grow up to hurt or kill the little innocent birds or abuse any of the poor dumb animals with which they may have to deal.

EVIL ASSOCIATIONS.—As already intimated, the early training of a child will have an important bearing upon his future character. If he is taught to be honest, truthful and pure while he is young, when he grows up he will be fortified and strengthened to resist the temptations of vice and immorality which will beset his path on every side. But if he gets his training on the streets and around the grog-shops, he will be sure to fall a victim to intemperance, vicious habits and sensuality. Parents and teachers, therefore, should guard well the avenues by which evil may approach the young mind, and erect barriers against vice by careful instruction and chaste examples. Protect him against evil associates, for it is among these that the first lessons in bad language are learned, and which are soon followed by impure thoughts and impure actions.

HAPPY HOMES.—Make the child's home a happy one; make it so attractive that he will prefer it to any other place. Give him a pleasant room in which to sleep, and supply him with good books, not love-sick novels, but such as will furnish the mind with food and pure thoughts. Cultivate music in the home; it has an inspiring and elevating influence upon both young and old; all children love music, and if they cannot find it at home will be likely to seek it elsewhere. The inquiring minds of children will be occupied in some way, and it is of the utmost importance that they should be early filled with thoughts that will lead them to pure and noble deeds; only in this way can the foundation be laid for that purity of character which alone will insure purity of life.

SCOLDING.—A great deal of injury is done to children by their parents' scolding. It sours their temper, so that one thorough scolding prepares the way for two or three more. The more you scold the more you will have to scold, because you will become crosser, and your children likewise.

Scolding alienates the hearts of your children. Depend upon it, they will not love you as well after you have berated them as they did before. You may approach them with firmness and decision, and they will feel the justice of your conduct and will love you, notwithstanding all; but they hate scolding. It stirs up the bad blood, while it discloses your weakness, and lowers you in their estimation. Their little hearts should be melted and molded with voices of kindness, so that they may go to their slumbers with thoughts of love stealing around their souls and whispering peace.

SEXUAL KNOWLEDGE.—Another most essential part of a child's early education is to teach him the relation which the Creator has established between the sexes. Hitherto this part of his early education has been almost totally neglected, the subject being regarded as too delicate or too sacred for his reception. Hence, he has been left to the tender mercy of ignorant servants and associates to give him this important information, and we see what the result has been. Certain it is that the stealthy approaches of vice have been fostered by the existing system. Now, as the child will obtain this knowledge from some source or other, it is infinitely better for him to receive it from his parents or some trustworthy friend, instead of being taught it by some vicious person.

The subject is one that should be handled with the greatest delicacy of expression, so as to avoid rousing morbid curiosity or stimulating the passions, special care being taken to train the child so that he will associate with the name of woman only pure, chaste and noble thoughts. The inquisitive mind and lively imagination of childhood are easily corrupted, while the seeds of vice will germinate and flourish in the soul and bear their hideous fruit in later years.

WHERE DOES THE BABY COME FROM?—Let no parent neglect, then, the sacred duty of teaching the child the mysteries of generation and the origin of life so far as these are known. The child will not long credit the story of the "doctor bringing the baby in his coat pocket," or its being "sent by angels." It will be better to tell the exact truth about this as of everything else the child has to learn in the world, of its sorrow and sin, of its joy and love. Don't put it off by telling it not to "ask such questions;" you are only telling it to go ask some one else, for it is bound to know all about it sooner or later. How much safer it will be for the child to receive this truth from the pure and loving lips of the father or mother in whom it can confide. Take its little hand, then, in yours, and explain to it that everything in the universe is created male and female. Not only men and women, but all animals, all birds, all fishes, and insects; even the trees and flowers. Every new life has its origin in the union of the sexes—male and female—and by this sexual union the male *sperm* comes in contact with the female *ovum* or egg, and a new being is created. Soon after conception, this *minute germ*—so small that it cannot be seen with the naked eye—takes up its abode in the mother's womb; here it is nourished by the mother's blood, and grows until it is too large for the little house where it has been staying for the last *nine months*, and it moves out and comes to live with us. This is the simple story about the baby, and "where it comes from." It is the way all animals that live in this world, such as little pigs, puppies, calves, lambs, etc., are "bred and born."

Teach the child, then, at an early period these important lessons concerning life and the relationship of the sexes. Parents or guardians are the proper persons to do this; do not turn the child over to some one else to give this information, if you do, it will most likely obtain it from vulgar schoolmates or through some other immoral or degrading channel, which you may have occassion to regret when it is too late. If our young people were made properly acquainted with the physiology of the sexual functions they would be far less likely to form habits of self-abuse, or be led astray by other corrupting influences.

THE EVIL EFFECTS OF ALCOHOL.

ANOTHER important part of a child's early education is to teach him to abstain from the use of alcoholic liquors. As already observed, the future character of an individual depends largely on his early training. If parents would have their child grow up pure, healthy and wise; if they would have him become a blessing instead of a curse; if they would save him from corruption and vice; if they would save him from a drunkard's career and a drunkard's grave, they must teach him to keep clear of the contaminating and seductive influences of alcoholic liquors. He should be taught by precept and example to shun the intoxicating cup, for "at last it stingeth like a serpent and biteth like an adder;" once imbibed, it may beget in him passions which he will never be able to control, and may become a curse to him as it is a desolating bane to society. If all parents would abstain from intoxicating liquors, and teach their children to do likewise, we would soon witness a glorious change. We should see every home made safer and happier; we should see the poor-houses empty and the jails desolate; we should see thousands of young men and maidens, instead of becoming victims of intemperance, delighting themselves in doing good and making others happy; we should see the very earth grow brighter and heaven come nearer, as the dark clouds of this national curse would take their departure.

But the practical question is, how shall we bring about this desirable result? So long as people drink we shall have drunkenness; let the habit be once formed and the victim is seldom reclaimed. Prevention is our only cure; and here, as everywhere in this erring and wicked world, we shall find "ignorance the evil, and knowledge the remedy." Our only faith and hope of banishing this evil are by placing before the world, and especially before the rising generation, the exact truth respecting the action of alcohol on the human system.

For centuries past some of the most erroneous and dangerous doctrines have been promulgated by the medical profession, and others, respecting the action and value of alcohol, and which have been the principal means of fostering and perpetuating intemperance. Rolla A. Law, a distinguished advocate of temperance, declared that in his experience with the rum fiend he found "alcoholic medication the chief obstacle in his pathway," and the "medical profession the stronghold of intemperance." And Dr. Juett, another eminent advocate, gave testimony to the same effect.

Everywhere the people are indoctrinated in the belief that alcohol is a "blood nutriment," that it "promotes digestion," that it "supports vitality," that it is a "fuel food," and that it is the "conservator of health." Now, if this doctrine be *true*, we can see no reason why alcohol should not be used *secundum artem;* indeed, a very large class of our fellow-citizens, recognizing these claims, do use it, believing it to be the conservator of health and the milk of human life. Many keep it on their tables, use it with their meals and train their children to believe in its magic powers.

The London *Lancet*, which is good authority on the subject, in answer to the question, "What quantity of alcohol may be taken daily with advantage?" replied, that, "being both a food and a stimulant, two glasses a day might be taken with *advantage.*" In a long article published in the New York *Times*, a few years ago, the writer, who professed to give "The last word of physiology to date" respecting the value of alcohol, said: "For those who are not blessed with total unconsciousness of a stomach and especially for elderly or delicate persons, digestion is made easier and more complete by the moderate use of wine or whisky taken at meals." As to the quantity, he says, "Dr. Parks put the limit of usefulness at from one to one and a half ounces of alcohol daily, a limit corresponding roughly to a pint of claret or other light wine, and twice as much of beer."

The above quotations are fair specimens of the alcohol doctrine as taught in the medical journals and text-books at the present day. And, we repeat, if it is correct that alcohol is a healthy food, if it will give strength to the weak and enfeebled body, if it will promote digestion and furnish heat for the system, then nearly everybody ought to use it, for nine-tenths of the people are suffering from a condition which calls for this supposed *elixir vitæ*. But let us carry the case to the Court of Fact, and let impartial reason decide this alcoholic food puzzle—" Three in one, and one in three."

In presenting the case to the court, the first question is, What is alcohol? And what are its effects on the human system? In chemical language, alcohol is a hydrated oxide of ethyl. It is a clear, volatile, inflammable liquid, and is the intoxicating principle in all spirituous liquors. It is nowhere to be found in nature, in anything which the Creator has made endowed with organism and life; it is a device of man, the offspring of death, evolved through the *destructive* process of *decomposition*. It is a *narcotic poison*, according to Orfila, Christinson, Taylor and Pereira; while others class it among the "*caustic-irritant*" poisons. When taken in large doses it destroys life very quickly. Persons have been known to die almost immediately after drinking from half a pint to a pint of ardent spirits. Dr. Percy, an eminent French surgeon, gave to a spaniel bitch two and a quarter ounces of alcohol. She immediately uttered a plaintive cry and fell helpless to the ground. "Never," says he, "did I see every spark of vitality more effectually and instantaneously extinguished. In less than two minutes not a single pulsation of the heart could be felt." Further experiments show that "it is inimical to everything that has life, either animal or vegetable." When "applied to the roots of plants or trees it destroys them in a short time." If it is taken into the mouth and held for a few minutes, it inflames and blisters the mucous membrane and deadens the sense of taste. If a piece of rag be saturated with it and applied to the skin, preventing evaporation by means of an oil-silk bandage, in a short time the part becomes hot, painful, inflamed and blistered as if burned. These experiments prove that alcohol is an *irritant poison.*"

When large doses are taken internally, the *primary* effect is to cause excitement of the nervous system, increased frequency of the pulse and a livelier flow of ideas, which are soon followed by a state of impaired perception and motor power; these are in turn followed by insensibility, unconsciousness and all the phenomena which accompany a fit of apoplexy. In all such cases the temperature of the body will be found to have fallen from 4° to 6° below the normal. After death all the large vascular organs are found engorged with blood, which will *furnish alcohol* by distillation. Alfred Swayne Taylor, the eminent toxicologist, says: "The stomach has been found intensely congested or inflamed, the mucous membrane being of a bright red or of a dark-brown color." "The brain and its membranes are congested, and, in some instances, there is effusion of blood or serum beneath the inner membrane, and in some cases the lungs and heart are found engorged with dark blood."

These are a few of the prominent symptoms induced and the morbid conditions observed upon the bodies of those who have suffered and died from the effects of large doses of alcohol. They clearly demonstrate the terrible results produced by this *poison* when taken into the human system. And the thought uppermost in every intelligent mind must be, why this *deadly poison* should be regarded as a "blood nutrient" and a "supporter of vitality." No such claims are made for opium, belladonna, hyoscyamus, stramonium, tobacco or any other narcotic poison; why then for alcohol?

Now, to understand the nature and functions of food, we must first understand the human body that needs food. And by the aid of chemistry and physiology we arrive at this knowledge. Chemically examined, we find the human body composed of a variety of compound substances, which are capable of being reduced to simpler forms. If we take a piece of human flesh we find it yields albumen, fibrine, gelatine, fatty matters, salts of soda, potash, lime, magnesia and iron; while the solids, as bone and other parts, contain, besides, a large percentage of gelatine, phosphate of lime, carbonate of lime, fluate of lime, phosphate of magnesia and a small portion of chloride of sodium. We also find that water enters largely into all the tissues of the body; it is the vehicle for conveying the nutritive material to all parts of the system and removing the products of waste as fast as formed.

Such, in brief, are the materials that compose the human body; and any article claiming to be food must contain one or more of these substances entering into its composition, or it must contain those elements in such a state of combination that the system can appropriate them to its own use. It is not what is taken into the stomach that nourishes the body, but what can be digested and worked up into living tissue and repair the waste that is continually going on in the vital organism. What, then, are those physiological operations which take place in the body that necessitate the use of food? The first in importance is that of *assimilation*, the process by which the body is nourished and repaired by food suitable for that purpose.

Another is that of *combustion*, by which the

body is preserved at a given temperature, 98½ degrees.

Another physiological process is that of *disintegration*, or the pulling down and change of structure that are continually going on within the body. We cannot utter a word or move a muscle but we wear away some portion of this delicate and complicated machine. And to repair this constant waste it is necessary to supply the system with new material from without.

Then again we have the process of *elimination*, by means of which those worn-out particles that can no longer be used for the purpose of life, and the retention of which would be a source of danger and disease, are expelled from the system. Every moment we live Nature is engaged in burning up or casting out the product of disintegration whereby the body is kept pure and healthy.

Having endeavored to explain the composition of the body and the physiological operations which take place necessitating food, we are prepared to inquire, *Is alcohol food?* And under this term we include all intoxicating liquors, because it is wholly on account of the *alcohol* they contain that such drinks are used; take it away and no one would think of drinking the disgusting residue.

Among the principal alcoholic beverages are brandy, whisky, rum, gin, wine, beer, ale, porter and cider. They are all essentially the same, the difference being only one of degree. For example, an imperial pint of *brandy* contains $9\frac{1}{2}$ ounces of water, $10\frac{1}{2}$ ounces of alcohol and 80 grains of burnt sugar, while *rum* contains 5 ounces of water and 15 ounces of alcohol. *Port wine* contains 16 ounces of water, 4 ounces of alcohol, 1 ounce of sugar and 80 grains of tartaric acid. *Beer* contains about 6 per cent. of alcohol, the balance water, a little gum, sugar and starch, which it holds in solution. These drinks contain besides the above a little coloring and flavoring matter. But do they contain the constituent elements of the body? Certainly not in any available form. They have no iron or salt for the blood, no gluten, phosphorus or lime for the bones, and no albumen—a substance which is the basis of every living organism.

How, then, can an article that is destitute of these essential elements nourish and repair the waste of the body? Now, it is a distinctive feature of food that it is used up in the system. In passing through the various changes it produces *force* and *heat*, is then reduced to lower and simpler forms and cast out as effete matter. But alcohol, when taken into the system, is eliminated from its precincts in the same condition as it enters. In proof of this it has been recollected from the breath, from the perspiration, from the secretions of the kidneys, and from the milk of nursing mothers who drank it. And, furthermore, chemistry has ransacked the innermost recesses of the human body to find the derivatives of alcohol—*aldehyde* and *acetic acid*—the substances into which it would turn if decomposed, but no traces of them have yet been found.

If, then, it will not stick to the living machine; if it is not a flesh-forming material; and if it will not furnish animal heat, but diminishes the temperature of the body, as demonstrated by innumerable experiments, what in the name of common sense and science does it do to justify the claim that it is a "blood nutrient" and a "supporter of vitality?"

Professor Yeomans, in his "Class-Book of Chemistry," says: "There is no evidence whatever that under any circumstances is alcohol capable of serving for animal nutrition."

Dr. Carpenter, the eminent physiologist, declares that "Alcoholic liquors cannot supply anything which is essential to the due nutrition of the system." Again, he says: "Wine is quite superfluous to man; it is continually followed by the expenditure of power."

Dr. Markham, Fellow of the Royal Society, sums up a long discussion on alcohol in the "British Medical Journal," as follows: "It is to all intents a foreign agent which the body gets rid of as soon as it can. It is not a supporter of combustion. Part, probably the whole of it escapes from the body, and none of it, so far as we know, is assimilated. It is, therefore, not a food in the eye of science."

But notwithstanding these facts, which have again and again been demonstrated, the supporters of alcohol are determined to have it perform some important part in the animal economy, and they declare that it "prevents tissue metamorphosis, and offers itself in the blood as a substitute for food." In other words, it stops the wear and waste that are continually going on in the body and compels the system to subsist upon *nothing*. And this is the latest and most advanced thought of the votaries of alcoholic food-action. It is the logical conclusion of nearly all of the medical journals and leading authors on materia medica in this country and in Europe. The late Dr. Anstie, M. R. C. P., declared that "Alcohol will not only support life, but even the bulk of the body for many days during the abstinence of common foods." According to this distinguished teacher, had Dr. Tanner drunk whisky instead of water he might have tipped the beam at 158 pounds at the end of his forty days' fast instead of 122 as the result proved. He might not have been quite so companionable to his immediate friends—with all those 36 pounds of worn-out and effete matter retained in his system—but, nevertheless, he would have had the *bulk* and weight all the same. Think of *venous* blood and foul secretions being retained in the body as a substitute for natural healthy food!

The clinical facts which some writers have produced as demonstrative of the food-action of alcohol are, as such, worth absolutely *nothing*. The proof here must be rigid—one of the scale-and-balance kind. Let us be told what the weight of the patient was *before* the experiment was commenced, and what *after*. Let us know how much water was taken *with* the alcohol, and be satisfied that nothing *but* diluted alcohols were swallowed while the experiments were going on. The analysis of such facts would enable us to arrive at something *positive* upon the subject. We have no hesitation in saying that to call alcohol food, or even a substitute for food, in the present state of our knowledge of its effects, is an *abuse* of knowledge. And those who affirm it to be should give something like a tangible proof of the fact. Let them show that a person fed *solely* on alcoholic liquor for ten or twelve days has gained, or at least not *lost*, in weight. To say that an emaciated creature who rises from a bed of sickness, and who has taken during his illness large quantities of alcohol *and* water, is a living proof that alcohol is food, or that it will in any way support life, is manifestly an unfounded assumption.

The claim that alcohol promotes digestion is equally delusive. It has been clearly demonstrated that instead of assisting, it actually arrests the process of digestion and prevents the assimilation of food. "It is a remarkable fact," says Dr. Dundas Thompson, "that alcohol, when added to the digestive fluid, produces a white precipitate, so that that fluid is no longer capable of digesting animal or vegetable matter."

Bowman and Todd, in their "Class Book of Chemistry," declare that "Alcohol retards digestion by coagulating the pepsin, an essential element of the gastric juice. Were it not that wine and spirits are rapidly absorbed, the introduction of these into the stomach in any quantity would be a complete bar to the digestion of food." As a proof of this declaration, if we take a vial containing gastric juice, and place in it some crumbs of bread and meat, keep it at a temperature of 98°, in a few hours it will be dissolved into a poultacious mass. If to another vial of gastric juice and food treated in the same way we add a small quantity of alcohol, the dissolving process will be arrested, and the food will remain unchanged for days.

In further confirmation of this fact, Dr. Figg "took two dogs and gave to each five ounces of cold roast mutton, cut into small squares and passed into the œsophagus without contact with the teeth. An elastic tube was passed into the stomach of one, and an ounce and a quarter of alcohol injected. After five hours both animals were killed. In the one where the meat had been taken by itself it had all disappeared. In the other, the meat was still in the stomach and the pieces were as angular as when swallowed."

Dr. Beddow, another eminent physician, made similar experiments on dogs, and found that "*three drachms* (less than than *three* teaspoonfuls) of alcohol completely arrested digestion for over four hours."

Does any one require stronger evidence than this that alcohol is not a promoter of digestion? With these facts staring us in the face, how can we reconcile the practice of physicians prescribing porter, ale, brandy and alcoholic liquors under the pretense of supporting the patient and assisting digestion?

Again, we are told that alcohol is a "fuel food," or "heat-forming material." This is a very popular belief indulged in, and is the legitimate offspring of the "blood-nutriment" and "life-supporting" theory which has been handed down as a traditional inheritance. It has entrapped many a poor fellow who has been made to sacrifice his health and very life on the altar of this false teaching. And what are the facts in the case? Here, again, we must put this alcoholic bull to the test of experiment; for only by experiment and careful observation can we ascertain the property of things and learn to correct false theories and erroneous conceptions.

It is generally conceded that animal heat is produced by the oxidation or combustion of the carbonaceous ingredients of the food and tissues. Now, as alcohol is not burned nor otherwise consumed in the system, but passes out of the body in the same condition as it enters (as is shown by being recollected from the mother's milk and other secretions of the body), the inference is plain that it is not a "fuel food." But if further evidence is needed to convince the "doubting Thomas," let him test the matter with a clinical thermometer;

place the bulb under the tongue, allow it to remain there from five to seven minutes; note the temperature; now take a glass of brandy, and after waiting fifteen or twenty minutes take the temperature again, and he will find that it has fallen in proportion to the amount and strength of spirits imbibed. Dr. Kirk, late Professor in the University of Edinburgh, says, "One glass of brandy will continue to lower the temperature for about four hours."

Prof. N. S. Davis, a prominent physician of Chicago, demonstrated as long ago as 1850 that the presence of alcohol in the system lowered the temperature. Since then he has fully established its correctness by a series of experiments performed with a delicately graduated thermometer, taking the temperature every half hour for three hours after the moderate use of wine and whisky.

Dr. C. Binz, a distinguished German physician, made numerous experiments with the view to determine the action of *non*-poisonous doses of alcohol upon the body. He found that "half a glass of light hock, or a small glass of cognac (these drinks contain about 10 per cent. of alcohol) caused a fall of from 0.4° to 0.6° in a very short time. In experiments made upon dogs with poisonous doses there was a fall in temperature of from 4° to 6° in from one to two hours." Dumeril, Dermarquay, Magnus, and others in Europe, experimented upon man and domestic animals and obtained similar results. The testimony of Sir James Ross, Sir John Richardson, Dr. Hayes, and other Arctic explorers, is that alcohol is not only useless, but positively injurious as respiratory or fuel food.

The claim that alcohol gives strength to the weak and enfeebled body is equally fallacious. It has been clearly demonstrated, not only by the foregoing investigations, but by scientific facts, that its presence in the system *diminishes* the *strength* and the power of endurance. The results of physical labor, as shown in the field, on the march, at the forge, in the workshop, and in all the physical and intellectual pursuits, prove that the spirit-drinker fails to cope with the *non-user* of alcohol.

Viewing the case then from whatever standpoint we may, we find it to be an agent foreign to the body of man, a poison of a most dangerous and fascinating character, the cautious use of which is always attended with risk, not only to man's physical constitution, but also to his moral and spiritual nature. He who uses these liquors, knowing them to be bad, adds to the violation of physical law, moral depravity, and he who uses them, ignorant of their properties, is now *inexcusable*. There was a period, before science had commenced her researches into this matter, when such ignorance was excusable; but we are now surrounded by light, and it is our duty as rational beings to make inquiry. Should we wilfully neglect to do this, and yet continue to use alcoholic poisons, then we knowingly commit a sin.

Those who use wines on their tables, and set the example of moderate drinking, delude and mislead thousands to their ruin. So far as example goes, the moderate drinker exerts a far more dangerous influence upon society than the poor drunkard. He gives an air of respectability to the practice, and thousands who attempt to follow his example fall by the wayside. But the drunkard excites our disgust, and we pass him by, and fear not the contaminating influence of his example.

And now, in taking leave of the subject, we desire to impress upon all parents the importance of teaching their children the exact truth respecting the action of alcohol on the human system. We have seen how persons have been deceived and misled regarding its value as a nutritive agent, as a promoter of digestion, as a supporter of vitality, and as a heat-forming material. And we have also seen how destructive it is to life and health, corrupting the blood, inflaming the tissues, and causing disease in every part of the body. And no less destructive is it to man's moral and spiritual well-being. By its action on the brain it dethrones reason, paralyzes the will, puts conscience to sleep, and stirs up all the vile and brutal passions in man's nature.

When the medical profession move in earnest and teach the exact truth in regard to alcohol, we shall have a public sentiment, and out of that sentiment will come law and an answer to the prayer, "Lord, that I might be healed."

THE TOBACCO HABIT.

It is a trite saying that "man is a creature of habit." And one of the most debasing and baneful habits to which he is addicted is that of smoking, chewing and snuffing tobacco. The effects are more insidious and the habit much stronger and more difficult to break off than that of using alcoholic liquors.

Nicotine, or the active principle of tobacco, is one of the most violent poisons known to man; like *prussic acid*, it destroys life in small doses and with great rapidity. This poison is found even in the *smoke* of tobacco, not being destroyed by combustion. In proof of this, if a current of smoke be passed through a vessel of water an oily substance will soon be found floating on the surface; if this be placed on the tongue of a cat, it will destroy the life of the animal very quickly. If the smoke from a pipe or cigar be concentrated on a sheet of paper, the deposit will be found to contain the same deadly poison. Hence, every person who respires the same, willingly or unwillingly, must have the blood in his veins more or less impregnated with the poison.

There are a great many foolish and absurd customs in this world, but we know of none so injurious and degrading as the tobacco habit. Among the savage tribes of the Rocky Mountains it is customary or fashionable to flatten their heads by long-continued pressure. In other barbarous countries they slit the ears and nose and hang from them tin, brass and other cheap ornaments. In China they compress the feet of the females from birth to prevent their growth. The Turks cram their women after the manner of stuffing geese, that they may become enormously fleshy. Some African tribes knock out their upper front teeth and otherwise disfigure their bodies; but none of these are so injurious and debasing as poisoning the system with alcohol and tobacco. We can excuse these poor semi-barbarians who flatten their heads, slit their ears, compress their feet, knock out their teeth and tattoo their skins; but for a highly civilized and

Christian people to poison their bodies, and corrupt their moral nature by the abuse of a deadly poison like tobacco, is quite incredible.

There are few persons who are not familiar with the injurious effects of smoking, chewing and snuffing; we have evidence of the fact all around us, and physicians of every school bear witness to the same; those who have fallen victims to the habit proclaim against it and regret that they ever commenced its use. We seldom meet a friend or patient who does not add his testimony to the mischief of which he has been the witness, in his own case or that of some friend, from tobacco. All medical authorities agree that the habitual use of it is injurious to man—physically, mentally and morally—causing various forms of disease. Says the "New York Medical Journal:" "In an experimental observation of thirty-eight boys of all classes of society and of average health, who had been using tobacco for periods ranging from two months to two years, twenty-seven showed severe injury to the constitution and insufficient growth; thirty-two showed the existence of irregularity of the heart's action, disordered stomachs, coughs and craving for alcohol; thirteen had intermittency of the pulse and one had consumption. After they had abandoned the use of tobacco, within six months one-half were free from all their former symptoms, and the remainder had recovered by the end of the year." Ought not these considerations to restrain every wise and good man from contracting or continuing such a senseless, destructive habit of self-indulgence?

The question is often asked, " Can a person who smokes tobacco be an honest and honorable man?" Here is the Hon. Neal Dow's answer: " In the street, on steamboats, in public places, in railway cars, everywhere, in fact, except in smoking-cars or in smoking-rooms, we have a right, all of us, to the free, fresh, pure air. This is as much our right as the purse in our pocket. No one has any more right to take it from us than to pick our pockets. To pick a pocket is stealing, robbery; what is it to take away the pure air from another, and to put stinking, poisoned air in its place?

"To sit beside another at the table and sprinkle his food with soot or asafœtida; what would such a procedure be called? What word is there in our language by which to characterize it? How would that differ from infusing a disgusting stench into the air for others to breathe? To poison another's food in that way would be called an intolerable abomination, and the doing of it would expose the party to a summary expulsion from decent society. But the poisoning of the air which others must breathe is so common a thing to do, so many persons practice it who would not pick a pocket, or poison other people's food, that most persons do not look upon it in its true light.

"I have often seen, in the streets, ladies and others walk very slowly or stop upon the sidewalk to allow the smoke to pass out of smelling distance. I have also seen people cross the street to avoid the stench of tobacco, which to many persons is intolerable. Have these people an undoubted right to the free, fresh air as they walk the streets? Then, what term are we to apply to the act of poisoning—for tobacco smoke is a poison—the air for them to breathe? How may we justly stigmatize those who do it?"

But what can we do? Tobacco confronts us wherever we go; it smokes on every corner like the reeking of a dung-hill; on the streets, in the highways, everywhere, men and boys puff their tobacco smoke in ladies' faces who have no protection; chewers eject the filthy juice on the sidewalk, floors of railway cars and other public places, greatly to the annoyance of all decent people; errand boys and boot-blacks form clubs of three or four, passing their pipe from mouth to mouth, in the secluded nooks of every alley. It is here that vice grows strong in company; it is here the little boy receives his first practical lesson in larceny from his more advanced confederates; it is here, around the pipe, young pickpockets congregate and board the train that leads to ruin.

That this is true no one can deny. It is a grave and important matter for parents to consider. If they will save their boys from the *tobacco vice*, there will be little danger of their becoming drunkards. For it is a well-known fact that not one in fifty who *abstains* from the use of tobacco drinks alcoholic liquors; whereas, nine out of ten who use tobacco use intoxicating liquors to a greater or less extent; the two vices seem to be almost inseparable. Smoking, especially, causes thirst and vital depression, to relieve which alcoholic stimulants are resorted to. And thus two of the most debasing habits and vices to which human nature can be degraded are indulged in to the injury of the individual, in shortening his life, and to the injury and ruin of his offspring.

An argument in favor of tobacco is deduced from the universality of the habit. All nations, it is said, use stimulants of some kind; hence, it is argued, they supply a natural want in harmony with the design of the Creator.

If this logic be sound, all that is necessary to justify any vice, as gambling, prostitution, drunkenness, or any abomination, is its general prevalence. But it is not true that tobacco supplies a *natural want*. The very fact that it poisons every one who first attempts to use it, is a proof to the contrary. It is disgusting in the highest degree to the natural appetite, and contrary to the unwritten law that forbids its use. If it supplies a natural want, pray, tell us, why women are exempt? Do they not require it? Are the burdens which they have to bear not equal to those of men? Look into the cottages of the poor; see the wife and the mother as she struggles on from day to day, and often through long weary nights, unsustained by luxuries or stimulants, while her rugged husband must have his rum and tobacco, not because it supplies a natural want, but a *morbid* craving fostered by habit.

Again, it is asserted that " tobacco cannot be a poison, or, if so, it must be a very slow one, for persons use it many years and live to old age." This kind of reasoning may satisfy those who wish to indulge in the morbid luxury, but, when considered from a scientific standpoint, is worth absolutely nothing.

Let us inquire, what is a poison? Toxicologists tell us it is "a substance which, when taken into the animal economy, acts *injuriously* on the textures of organs." If the oil of tobacco, which is the active principle, be placed on the tongue of a cat or a dog, it will kill the animal in three or four minutes. This fact has been demonstrated by repeated experiments made by Professor Mussey, Drs. Brodie, Lizars and other experimentalists. Dr. Pereira, a distinguished author, states that an infusion of thirty grains of *crude* tobacco, administered as an injection, proved rapidly fatal; and numerous instances of a similar kind are reported by other writers. The "National Dispensatory," the highest authority in this country, says: "'Tobacco is hostile to all forms of vegetable or animal life." Again, it says: "Habitual smoking, snuffing or chewing lessens the natural appetite, impairs digestion, irritates the mouth and throat, rendering it habitually congested, and destroys the purity of the voice. It induces an habitual sense of uneasiness and nervousness, and palpitation of the heart. Chewing causes gastralgia, and smoking neuralgia. In numerous instances it has produced *amaurosis*."

After death from tobacco, "the brain is found empty of blood, the stomach reddened in round spots and raised, resembling patches of dark velvet; the blood is dark and fluid; the lungs are pale, while the heart is engorged with blood."

These facts prove, beyond a question of

doubt, that tobacco is a poison, potent and pernicious. It also proves that it cannot be taken into the system in any appreciable quantity without doing injury. The fact that the human organism has the capacity to accommodate itself in a wonderful degree to the use of poisons, if the quantity taken only be *gradually* increased, is no proof that they are not injurious to the system. All poisons are cumulative in their actions; that is, small doses, frequently repeated, injure the body and finally destroy life as completely as though a poisonous dose had been taken at once; but, of course, the action extends over a longer period. Hence, tobacco, being a poison and foreign to the body, the *direction of the action must be the same* and the result alike disastrous.

But, some one says, "My father used tobacco nearly all his life and lived to be an old man; therefore, it cannot be so *very* injurious." Well, we have known some persons to be diseased nearly all their lives and yet live to old age. Is that any proof that disease is not *hurtful* and that it does not shorten human life? Why should the *tobacco* disease not injure the system the same as any other disease? Do not both poison the life-blood and produce disorder and death? To say that a man who chews or smokes a ton of tobacco and lives to be seventy-five years old would not have lived longer and been better without it, is an unfounded assumption. The only way by which to prove the truth or falsity of such a proposition would be to select, say, one thousand young men of the same age, free from disease and all taint of alcohol and tobacco, place them under the same favorable circumstances as regards diet, exercise and hygienic conditions, except that one-half of them shall have full swing at the best brands of " pig-tail " or " fine-cut tobacco." At the end of a hundred years, more or less, take an account of stock, and if it is found that those who use tobacco maintain the same high standard of health and length of life as those who do not use it, we shall have to acknowledge that tobacco is not a poison injurious to man, but a *morbid* luxury, and that the most to be said against it is that it is a dirty, filthy, degrading vice, obnoxious to the finer sensibilities of all decent people.

THE OPIUM BONDAGE.

WE cannot close this chapter on the training of children without a few warning words against the use of *opium*.

This drug has been long and extensively used as a medicine. Taken in a moderate dose, it produces exhilaration and pleasant flights of fancy, followed, in the course of an hour, by a disposition to sleep; or, if sleep does not take place, the body and mind enjoy a sense of repose from external impressions, while the mind is filled with dreamy and generally pleasant ideas. This condition of tranquillity and comfort may last for several hours, or sooner or later pass into a quiet sleep. Some headache, nausea and lassitude may follow the awakening, but these vary much with the dose and the individual. When a large dose has been taken it causes little or no excitement, but almost immediately reduces the frequency of the pulse, diminishes muscular power, causes giddiness and drowsiness, succeeded by insensibility and deep apoplectic sleep with loud snoring respiration, and the person dies in a few hours if not relieved.

Opium, as we have said, is used extensively in medicine, and is given for the relief of pain and to induce sleep. It gives temporary relief by benumbing the sensibilities of the patient so that he does not feel the pain; but the disease may run its course—even to a fatal termination—while the patient and his friends may not be aware of it. In transient diseases, and where the drug is not continued beyond a few days, the patient may not be *entrapped* by its seductive powers; but in diseases of a chronic or tedious character, like neuralgia, rheumatism and some nervous affections, where its use is continued beyond a few weeks, the patient is almost sure to fall a victim to the opium habit.

In this country the habit is rarely acquired except by first using it as a medicine, and it is largely extended beyond its legitimate use by being administered to infants by monthly nurses or ignorant, idle and unnatural mothers, in the form of "Paregoric," "Godfrey's Cordial," "Soothing Syrup," etc., etc. In consequence, thousands of these little ones suffer from almost constant narcotism, and thousands are annually poisoned in their cradles, their pure instincts perverted, their appetites depraved and their whole organisms debauched for life by these pernicious compounds.

A case which recently came under our care will serve to illustrate the wretched condition of one of these little victims. The history of the case is as follows: Soon after the child was born it was fed on sweetened water, and in a short time it became fretful and cried as if in great pain; the nurse gave it *catmint tea*, but to little purpose, as the suffering and crying continued; *laudanum* was next given in drop doses, which afforded temporary relief, the colic, however, recurred from day to day, and the laudanum was continued. After pursuing this treatment for several weeks "Mrs. Winslow's Soothing Syrup" was substituted for the laudanum. Thus matters went on from better to worse for nearly three months. The family physician was now called in, and he prescribed *laudanum*, which was given *secundum artem* up to the time of our first visit.

The infant was now five months old and taking *twenty drops* of laudanum twice a day. This quantity, however, did not relieve its sufferings, and the doctor ordered *thirty* drops to be given at a dose. It was a most pitiable looking object of " death-in-life; " its body was emaciated to a skeleton, its skin was a dirty yellow and hung in folds on its trembling limbs; its big glassy eyes were sunk deep in their orbits; it started at the slightest noise, and clutched continually with its hands as if it was in the greatest agony.

We explained to the parents that this was a clear case of poisoning, and that it was a subject for legal investigation; that it looked to us like a conspiracy on the part of the doctor, mother and nurse to destroy the child, and we could not see why they were not all liable to arrest; for if it was not a case of willful poisoning it was at least one of *mal*-practice, which is no less an indictable offense. But, as might be expected, the perpetrators of this crime were allowed to escape, like thousands of others who commit similar acts upon their innocent offspring.

In this case, however, the use of the opium was discontinued by gradually diminishing the size of the dose, and at the end of two weeks of anxiety and suffering the child was free from the poisonous drug and well on his way to recovery. He began to take food with a relish and to thrive and was happy. To-day he is a bright, lively boy; but if he lives to manhood without becoming addicted to the habit of using tobacco and rum, he will be the eighth wonder of the world.

The use of opium is also increasing to an alarming extent among our adult population. We are acquainted with a score or more confirmed opium-eaters who take it in the form of laudanum, morphia and the crude drug. They commenced the habit in every instance by first using it as a medicine. In many cases it will give temporary relief at first, but it will not cure or do any permanent good, but will often fix the disease, as it were, and make it more difficult to cure. It is a thousand times better to *endure* pain, even for days, than be entrapped by an enemy which comes in the garb of an angel with its balmy powers, but which will ultimately bind its victim in chains which will "drag him down to the depths of an awful hell."

Who, then, is safe that takes opium even under

the direction of a physician? A few days ago a former patient called on me and related his experience with this god of dreams. "Some six months ago," said he, "I was attacked with a rheumatic pain in the shoulder, which annoyed me for a week or two, but did not interfere particularly with my business; one day it became more intolerant, and I called in the doctor; he deliberated a moment, and then took out his hypodermic syringe, and injected a dose of morphia into my arm; in a few minutes I was free from pain, and was soon asleep; next day the pain was as bad as ever, and the doctor gave me another injection of morphia, and I slept all night; again the pain recurred, and the drug was repeated. This method of treatment was kept up for nearly six weeks, when the pain subsided, and I relinquished the morphia. Now a conflict ensued which I had not even dreamed of: I found myself the slave of a tyrant, which I had no power to control, and I was wretched beyond anything I had ever experienced. My appetite was gone; my nerves were all unstrung, and sleep was impossible; I would spring out of bed at night and pace the room like a madman; I had little control of my will-power, and was a terror to my family. For two mortal weeks this struggle continued before I could say that

I was free from this tyrant who in so short a time had bound and made me an abject slave.

This is but a miniature picture of the horrible nightmare which this drug is capable of producing. To fully understand the bewitching and all-absorbing power of morphia on the human system, after the habit has been firmly established, one should read the

CONFESSION OF AN OPIUM SLAVE.—Mrs. James Havens, Lecturer on Narcotics in the W. C. T. U., relates a portion of a confession made by an opium slave, which we take the liberty to copy for the benefit of those who wish to learn the power and influence of morphia on the human system.

"I was engaged in journalism in an Eastern city at a salary which I thought justified me in the most arduous labor. I was ambitious to succeed as a journalist, and I worked beyond my strength, paying little heed to the warning of my overwrought nerves and weary brain, until they finally rebelled and called a halt. But rest was not to be thought of in my case, and I hastened to our old family physician and friend for advice. I rebelled at his imperative prescription of 'Rest,' and impatiently demanded a tonic that would revive my failing energies; so he decided to test the effect of morphia upon me. He said nothing to me, however, of the proposed experiment, and, as I had always trusted to his skill and judgment, I made no inquiries.

"Under the influence of the delightful panacea I worked with redoubled zeal. My brain grew luminous with beautiful imagery, my thoughts flew with lightning speed, and work was the most delightful pastime. I joyfully listened to the commendations of my friends for the elegance and profusion of my literary labors.

"But when the mysterious panacea had spent its power I was wretched beyond description. My nerves quivered, my limbs trembled, and my teeth chattered as if with an ague chill. Of course I immediately applied for another prescription of the magical powders, which was granted under protest. It seems strange to me now that I never cared to inquire the name or nature of the drug until I had been under its influence for a succession of weeks. One day the physician suggested the propriety of preparing the powders myself, as I was so determined to have them, and produced a tiny, blue-wrapped bottle labeled '*Morphia sulph.*' A shuddering horror seized me. I knew that whatever the powders were it was impossible to live without them, but I never dreamed they were morphia. I was fearfully alarmed, and exclaimed in dismay, 'Can it be possible, doctor, that I have become a slave to opium?' 'Oh,' replied my physician, placidly, 'Not that bad, we hope;' then added, sternly, 'I prescribed those powders as a remedy for your nervousness, and I regret to know you have resorted to them as a stimulant.'

"But he quieted my fears, cautioned me to use great care and judgment in the frequency of its use, and never to take it unnecessarily. From that moment my doom was sealed, and the signet of inexorable fate was stamped upon it. After again repeating his words of caution the physician placed the bottle of morphia in my hands and left me alone and powerless to the mercy of a demon. Ah! I have seen the time since then that the most merciful prayer my lips could utter was that he, my good friend (?) and trusted physician, might suffer for one brief hour one tithe of the unutterable agony that I was compelled to endure for long, weary years. Thus left alone to the guidance of my own judgment—holding in my own hand the weapon that could successfully combat every adverse influence and brighten even the poorest joys of life, and with the assurance that no harm could befall if used judiciously—is it any wonder that I fell a willing victim to a power whose clanking chains I could only hear softly and sweetly low as the tinkle of a silver bell? Is it any wonder that I turned away with a sense of loathing and disgust from the prosy, commonplace scenes of everyday life when I held in my own hand the 'open sesame' to the whole vast fields of ideality—to roam at will through its enchanted palaces, to drink of the waters far sweeter than the 'nectar of the gods,' and eat of the fruit fairer and more delicious than ever grew on the health-giving trees of the garden of Paradise? How was I to know that those delicious waters would eventually pall upon my taste like the 'bitter waters of Marah,' and the luscious fruit, like the 'apples of Sodom,' turn to scorching, blistering ashes upon my lips?

"After the physician left me to the dictates of my own judgment, there was not a single moment for five long years that I was not under the weird and witching power of morphia. It is true, I made many a wretched attempt to free myself, but the miserable sensation caused by the fading influence of the drug was too terrible to be borne. The first two years of the five were all one blissful, roseate dream—not a pain—not a grief or a sorrow could by any means approach me, and I daily experienced a vivid sense of the expansion of all my powers. Whatever duty I had to perform, domestic, social or intellectual, I felt fully equal to the task. My literary labors were extended far into the night without cessation, yet I experienced no fatigue. Neither hunger, thirst, sleep nor weariness made any demands upon my system. Four hours of fitful slumber out of the twenty-four were all I required, and, in fact, I could do very well without that.

"Every habit of my life paid exorbitant tribute to the baleful extortioner. At the expiration of about two years, very slowly, and by almost imperceptible degrees, a change came over my unnatural life. A shadowy gloom, a darkening terror began to envelop my spirits—black, horrible forebodings began to oppress me. An ever-present consciousness of some awful impending doom weighed like a deadly nightmare upon my soul, and, like the 'old man of the sea,' it could not be shaken off. Day and night alike I was compelled to endure the ghastly burden of the consciousness that the culminating horrors of the dreaded doom were drawing nearer and nearer with the dawning of every morning and the setting of every sun. I tried to imagine myself insane, knowing well that in such an event this horrible incubus was not real, but existed only in a diseased imagination. But in vain. I knew too well that I was now reaping as I had sown. I knew too well that I was the abject slave of a tyrant who had enticed me within the gates of Paradise only till the chains were welded to drag me, helpless and hopeless, down to the lowest depths of an awful hell.

"My literary work, which had previously been my delight, began now to be almost repulsively distasteful. At occasional intervals I tried to rally and believe that my work would soon regain its wonted charm, but too late! The brilliancy and the purity of my style had fled, and I found to my dismay that my pen had lost its cunning and my brain its accustomed poise! Frightened at the piteous wreck of my mental powers, and the failing of all my finer faculties, I made a thousand weak endeavors to free myself from my fatal hallucination, but the fetters were stronger than chains of brass, and my efforts were abortive.

"I appealed frantically to Heaven, but my prayers were impious, and only rebounded, unanswered, upon my own soul. At length remorse, the most pungent and exquisitely intolerable agony of all the tortures of the rack that opium has prepared for its victims, began eating its way into my soul. I looked backward with an irresistible longing to the time when I was free as other people; then I looked forward into the dreary, desolate future, so ghastly in its prospective horrors, with a shrinking, quivering dread that could not be appeased.

"Fear was the next emotion that most bitterly assailed me, and while remorse was still true to its fiendish trust, fear shook its quivering, palsied finger in my face and pointed to the frightful quicksands in my path. It was not a sudden, startling fear, but a constant, oppressive apprehension of evil, causing me to tremble at every sound and shiver at every breath. At length existence became so miserable that this life was no longer endurable, and I determined to end it by unlocking the portals of eternity with my own hands. I was well satisfied that eternity could hold no horrors superlative to this, and I even indulged a faint hope that the change might be beneficial. I had been told by my medical adviser that I could never break the chains that bound me and live; and so that was to be the manner of my exit, for I had determined to break my bonds even if death should be the result. Accordingly, I set my house in order and made every preparation for a long, long journey, and the struggle began.

"But oh, God of mercies! did ever death and life have a fiercer struggle? Hand to hand with the dread monster I battled for long, frightful weeks, just on the verge of Death's awful abyss, knowing that at any moment he might push me over. Nothing on earth, nothing in the unknown hereafter, could exceed the intolerable horrors of that unusual conflict. I had panoplied myself with one weapon, which, combined with my own will-power, was my whole armor of defense. That weapon was a solemn vow to the Almighty that if Heaven would assist me in my efforts I would help myself.

"I had often prayed for release unconditionally, but now I was willing to do my utmost in this unequal battle for freedom. With that vow upon my soul I could not retract, and, in fact, I felt a grim satisfaction in testing the remnant of my will-power to its utmost capacity, or, rather, to see which was the stronger, Death or I. For that purpose I placed a full, unopened bottle of morphia upon my table at the commencement of the struggle. I was true to my vow. I did exert my will-power, and I did conquer at last.

"But oh! I would have given a thousand worlds, were they mine, to have had that solemn vow blotted out, that I might die an easier death. Tortured with agony no language could express, I paced the dreary circuit of my room long, wretched days, and longed for night; but when the night closed in—those endless nights—I shrieked with frantic fear, and longed for day! Delirium, with its untold horrors, threw its weight into the scales against me. There was nothing fiendish or demoniac that was not brought into requisition by the opposing power.

"The ghastliest horrors of Dante's hideous imagery were, in comparison, but as flowery episodes in the journey of a lost soul through the rayless, pathless blackness of the dread Inferno! Thus, for weeks and months the unequal conflict continued, and it ofttimes seemed as if worn-out Nature would succumb. But the all-prevailing power of God's wondous grace, combined with the mighty strength of a determined *will*, won the victory, and *I am free!*"

Reader, this is a truthful picture of the terrible effects of opium after it once gets possession of its victim. Those who have ever been under its controlling influence can fully realize how every faculty of the mind is made subservient to its power. This example of one who has been reclaimed from its bondage should serve as a warning voice to all who may be tempted to use this dangerous drug even as a medicine, for while it will at first dispel pain and promote sleep, it will ultimately insinuate itself into every fiber of the body and inflict upon its victim the torments of the damned.

CHAPTER XIV.

MASTURBATION—SELF-ABUSE—SECRET VICE.

Prevalence of the Vice—Signs by which it can be Detected—Terrible Results of—Effects on Future Generations—A Cause of Defective Vision—Preventive Measures—Obscene Literature—The Cure of the Vice—Dietetic Measures.

Few persons, except medical men, have any just conception of the fearful prevalence and consequences of this vice—masturbation. It pervades all classes and conditions of society, from the lowest to the highest; even children as young as four to six years and upward are numbered among its victims, and are being carried by it to the very verge of moral and physical ruin. Those who practice it are often more unfortunate than guilty, inheriting, as they often do, a preponderance of the animal passion, which leads them to commit this crime against nature. Five children in every ten, over twelve years of age, bear the marks which this disgusting vice stamps on their countenance as a proof of their guilt. It is a crime that brings its own punishment—a sin that nature cannot forgive. Few of either sex escape this pollution, and the extent to which it prevails in our public schools and colleges is shocking beyond measure. It is in these institutions that the habit is formed early in life by being communicated from one to another. A single boy or girl may in a very short time corrupt a whole school despite the utmost care and vigilance on the part of parents or teachers. Thousands of children get their first lesson in this pernicious and debasing practice through evil associates at these institutions. Little boys and girls allowed to sleep with servants and nurses are often initiated into this practice by these caretakers, who manipulate their genital organs, either to gratify their own sensuality or to appease the children when they are cross or peevish. The practice is sometimes induced in little girls by *uncleanliness* or eruptions irritating the parts and compelling the friction which results in the unnatural gratification. The filthy vice thus early begun is sure to result in masturbation, which sooner or later leads these little ones to their ruin. No habit acquires such irresistible force by indulgence, and none entails such dreadful consequences on its votaries.

SIGNS BY WHICH THE VICE CAN BE DE-

TECTED.—Few persons are familiar with the signs by which this vice can be detected, nor do they fully realize the magnitude of the evil resulting from the practice. Among the prominent symptoms that manifest themselves in this species of sensuality may be noted the following: the child or young man or young woman betrays a sort of *bashfulness;* cannot bear to be looked at; face pale with a besotted expression; eyes weak with impaired vision; loss of memory and mental power; absent-minded; easily embarrassed; irritable temper; indisposed to any active exertion; headache; weakness and pain in the small of the back; feebleness of the whole body; emaciation and loss of appetite. Finally, when a young man has gone to a certain extent in this practice he loses all the natural desire for woman, and even the power to enjoy the pleasure of love. On the other hand, a young woman who has exhausted her vitality by self-abuse is often so virtuous as to hate the very sight of man and to loathe the very thought of sexual union. It is just such persons as these who are ever ready to condemn the poor girl who yields to the supplications of her lover and her own natural desires; they would treat her with indifference and banish her from their own pure society.

Terrible Effects of Self-Abuse.—It is the testimony of eminent physicians and authors that the sin of self-pollution or masturbation is one of the most destructive evils ever practiced by fallen man. "However revolting to the feelings it may be," says Sir W. C. Ellis, "to enter upon such a subject, it cannot be passed over in silence without a great violation of duty. Unhappily, it has not been hitherto exhibited in the awful light in which it deserves to be shown. *The worst of it is that it is seldom suspected.* There are many pale faces and languid, nervous feelings attributed to other causes, when all the mischief lies here."

Dr. Adam Clark says: "In many respects it is several degrees worse than common whoredom, and has in its train more awful consequences. It excites nature to undue action, and produces violent secretions which necessarily and speedily exhaust the vital principle and energy; hence the muscles become flaccid and feeble, the tone and natural action of the nerves relaxed and impeded, the understanding confused, the memory oblivious, the judgment perverted, the will indeterminate and wholly without energy to resist; the eyes appear languishing and without expression, and the countenance vacant; the appetite ceases, for the stomach is incapable of performing its proper office; nutrition fails; tremors, fears and terrors are generated, and thus the wretched victim drags out a miserable existence."

Another writer and distinguished lady says: "There is reason to believe that in nine cases out of ten those unhappy females who are tenants of houses of ill-fame have been victims of this vice in the first place. Were this the peculiar vice of the low and vulgar, there might be more excuse for the apathy and false delicacy that pervade the community respecting it. But it invades all ranks. Professed Christians are among its victims."

Says the "Boston Medical and Surgical Journal:" "A great number of the evils which come upon the youth at and after the age of puberty arise from masturbation, persisted in so as to waste the vital energies and enervate the physical and mental powers of man."

Its Effect upon Future Generations.—The above is a fair picture of the mental and physical ruin, in extreme cases, resulting from this sinful practice against nature. But the effects of it do not cease with the individuals who practice it, but are visited upon their children in the form of a feeble constitution, which renders them more liable to suffer and die from the diseases of childhood. And the habit, by impairing the vigor and vitality of the system, renders the individual far more liable to be attacked by any inflammatory or epidemic disease, and far more liable to die of such disease than an individual of virtuous habits.

Many suppose the injurious effects of self-abuse arise from a loss of the seminal fluid; but while this is certainly exhausting it is by no means the principal source of evil. Boys secrete no semen before puberty, and girls never any; therefore, the morbid condition observed in youths who practice this vice cannot be attributed to this cause. The real source of mischief is in the nervous orgasm which often amounts to almost a spasm, and when frequently repeated the nervous power is completely exhausted. No part of the organism suffers so much as the nervous system does from this sinful indulgence. It is a fruitful source of insanity, idiocy, *failing sight* and consumption in the young. It impairs every faculty of the mind and body, and leaves the poor victim to drag out a miserable existence as long as life lasts.

ITS EFFECT UPON THE EYES.—The question is daily asked, "Why do so many young people wear glasses nowadays?" In the little town where we reside there is a population of about fourteen hundred; out of this number not less than twelve per cent., who have not seen their thirty-fifth birthday, are suffering from defective vision, and are compelled to wear glasses, many of them little boys and girls under twelve years of age. Twenty years ago to have met a little boy or girl on the street, not ten years old, wearing spectacles, would have been taken as a childish joke or regarded as a natural curiosity, but at the present time they are common everywhere. If the demand for spectacles should increase in the same ratio for the next twenty-five years as it has done in the past twenty-five, we shall become such a "*spectacle*" as Alessandro di Spina, the Monk, never dreamed of.

But, in all soberness, what is it that compels so many of the young people to wear glasses? What has "got the matter with the peoples' eyes?" is a question that confronts us on every side. All authorities are agreed, from Galen down to the present time, that excessive sexual indulgence and solitary vice are a fruitful source of *nervous exhaustion* and *defective* vision. Now, as the organs of vision are made up largely of the optic nerves, which are the nerves of essential sensibility of sight, it can readily be seen that whatever tends to exhaust the nervous power must necessarily *impair* and *injure* the sense of vision. The diseases known as "*astigmatism*," "*amaurosis*," and other nervous affections of the eyes, so familiar to specialists, are caused, as we believe, by abuse of the sexual functions. That *narcotic stimulants*, tea, coffee and tobacco, play an important part in this matter there can be no reasonable doubt, but chief among them all is the one we have described. We do not mean to say that every one who is compelled to wear glasses is a *libertine* or an *onanist*, but, as the sins of the parents are visited on the children to the third and even fourth generation, the innocent have to suffer along with the guilty; and, while we are loth to admit the fact, it is nevertheless true that the cause of the defective vision, which necessitates the wearing of glasses by so many of the young people, is superinduced by excessive sexual indulgence and solitary vice. And if we are ever to get rid of this *blindness*, we must remove the primary or producing cause. Wearing spectacles will never cure it, neither will it save us from the moral degradation to which this vice inevitably leads.

PREVENTION BETTER THAN CURE.—How shall we cure this diseased manifestation and prevent all these horrible consequences from which civilization suffers from center to circumference? Prevention here is the all important thing. Young children who are ignorant of this vice should be kept so until they are old enough to understand how injurious and sinful the practice is. During this period the child's actions should be watched with scrupulous care, and if a tendency be observed to carry the hand to the genital organs, it must be taught that the habit is an evil one and must not be fostered. It should be taught from the beginning that it is wrong, immodest and fraught with danger to handle these parts, and if the habit is persisted in, it may be necessary to have night dresses made, closed like drawers, so that no mischievous handling is possible. Many wise mothers think it is best to make *all* night dresses in this way for children of both sexes until they are quite large.

As soon as the child is old enough to understand the subject, it should be taught by its parents or guardian the use and functions of the generative organs, and the serious consequences resulting from their abuse. The sooner this information is imparted to the child the better, while it has unlimited confidence in its natural protectors. Depend upon it, the best and the only safeguard to chastity is knowledge. Thousands of poor children of both sexes are corrupted and ruined from sheer ignorance. The boy who has been instructed in regard to the nature and evils of vice is warned and armed against it. The girl who understands the physiology of the sexual organs will neither plunge into solitary debauchery, nor can she be seduced, as is the ignorant girl, who falls a victim to some artful man, in a moment of passionate weakness, before she knows what she is doing. Be assured that knowledge is the safeguard of purity. It will act as "a lamp to the feet and a light to the path," and will enable them to escape the moral and physical ruin wrought through the agency of this terrible vice.

OBSCENE LITERATURE.—One of the most potent agents of evil, and one which contributes more largely towards inflaming the animal passions and fostering secret vice than any other, is the distribution and reading of obscene literature. It is terrible to contemplate the nature and extent of this filthy, deadly poison. The existence of such literature has been traced to schools and colleges in nearly all the States and Territories in the Union. Dealers in this detestable business have organized circulating libraries under the charge of the most vicious men and boys, who are paid to sell these obscene books, pamphlets, pictures and other articles too indecent to mention. Tons of this vile stuff are manufactured in

New York and other cities every month, and sent out all over the country, where it corrupts and ruins the purest and fairest sons and daughters of our land. We do not believe that parents are aware of the *danger* to which their children are exposed by this source of contamination, and they cannot be too vigilant in guarding against these "baits of the devil."

There are various ways by which this moral pestilence is disseminated. First, by obtaining the addresses of scholars and students in our schools and colleges and then sending their circulars to the victims. Then, again, under the pretense of taking a census of all the *unmarried* people, they offer to pay so much for a list of all such names as are sent. In this way they secure the addresses of thousands of innocent persons to whom they send catalogues, and too often receive letters in return from students of both sexes ordering these obscene books and other articles of an immoral character. Could anything be fraught with greater *danger* to the health and morals of a community than the spread of this vile literature? Cholera or yellow fever is as a cipher compared with this human pestilence, which destroys not only soul and body, but transmits to posterity the seeds of corruption which will flourish and bear fruit—after its own kind—for ages to come.

It may well be doubted whether any one factor contributes so largely to *sexual immorality* as the reading of obscene literature. By harboring lewd thoughts and conjuring up visions of nude women the individual exhausts his or her vitality to the extent of giving way to actual indulgence. The perusal of such books only tends to foster and keep alive this species of sensuality, which is well nigh universal among the youth of both sexes, and absorbs not only their waking thoughts, but their dreams at night as well. So long as our thoughts are lustful we are indulging in sexual abuse, and are almost sure, when temptation is presented, to commit the overt act of sin. If, then, we desire to live honest, virtuous lives, we shall have to banish all evil thoughts from our minds and keep our bodies pure also.

THE CURE FOR SELF-ABUSE.—When the habit is fully formed and is producing its terrible effects upon mind and body the question will naturally arise, what can be done to arrest and cure this evil? The answer is: moral suasion, hygienic regimen and appropriate medical treatment.

In the first place, the patient should be made acquainted with the enormity and terrible consequences of the vice. He or she must be encouraged in the most loving manner, by every motive of hope of manhood and womanhood, to *abandon* the practice. Unless this is given up at once, all other efforts will be in vain. It may require a hard struggle to effect this, but by persevering efforts victory will be certain. One very important element of success in breaking up this habit is in restraining the thoughts from all lascivious subjects. It is principally in the *mental* field where the battle must be fought, and where victory will be won or lost. Secret vice begins in the thoughts or imagination, and we shall not be likely to vanquish this *monster* unless we make the thoughts a special point of attack; and while it may be difficult at first to disperse the enemy, with a determined effort we shall succeed. The reading and perusal of obscene literature and exciting novels—to which reference has been made—should be scrupulously avoided, as they only tend to influence the passions.

In all bad cases, where the habit overpowers reason, the patient should not be left alone night or day. He should sleep on a hard bed or mattress, with light coverings, and in a *well-ventilated* apartment. He should arise as soon as awake in the morning and take a cold bath. He should take active exercise in the open air at some kind of work which will cause fatigue every day. He should choose for companions refined, intelligent and pure-minded men and women.

DIETETIC PRECAUTIONS.—The question of diet is one of no mean importance in the treatment of this "*disease without a name*," for "it has been proved beyond a doubt that the excitability and intensity of sexual passion are largely dependent upon what we eat and what we drink." Therefore, the diet should be plain but nutritious; very little animal food should be taken; bread made of unbolted wheat flour, oatmeal, potatoes, cracked wheat and fruit are proper articles. Take no oysters, rich fish, pork, fat and salted meats, pastry, sweetmeats and stimulating condiments, pepper, mustard, catsup, or even salt, except in moderate quantities. Avoid all *alcoholic* and *malt liquors, tea, coffee* and *tobacco* in all forms. Let the drink be *pure fresh water*, taken freely, especially on retiring at night.

Sobriety, then, in eating and drinking, together with a vigorous, prayerful effort to correct past errors and wrong-doing, will always be rewarded with success. If we desire a true manhood or womanhood, if we desire to be clean and virtuous, then we must keep our thoughts pure as well as our bodies. Mental purity is the most potent safeguard against lust and immorality. Therefore, if we wish to forsake this destructive vice and return to true morals and manhood, we must fly from occasions that provoke evil thoughts, avoid all parties and places where half-dressed women exhibit themselves, and where sensual excitations must shake our wavering determination. We should avoid all bad company and the tables of high-livers, where the fumes of tobacco and exciting wines are incessant solicitations to sensuality.

These are the obligations of which experience has demonstrated the necessity, and, if they are clearly recognized and intelligently applied, will lead to the restoration of health, and, we humbly trust, to a purer and more harmonious development of our lives.

GENERAL CONCLUSIONS.

THE result of the foregoing conclusions may appear small as regards the amount of novel information which has been disclosed, but we venture to think that the average reader will receive a little light in some dark places by the perusal of what we have written. There are those, no doubt, who will find some things here which are contrary to their preconceived opinions; but, remember, that what we sometimes cherish as truth is often most hurtful and very erroneous.

It has been our endeavor to show that the habits and conditions of life, the uses and abuses to which men and women have subjected their minds and bodies, have been to lower the standard of health, foster disease and entail it upon posterity. For centuries past we have been living out of the natural order, and as a consequence the people everywhere are suffering for the " sin of being sick."

Without a full observance of the laws of health we are all liable to ugliness, deformity, pain and every form of misery, all of which are included in the idea of disease. These conditions of health cannot be observed if they are not understood. We have so violated the laws of life, so neglected a knowledge of ourselves, so far gone astray from nature, that a pure, simple, natural life is not to be found among us.

The diseases and excessive mortality among infants, which we witness around us, are to a very large extent directly or indirectly attributable to the ignorance and conduct of the parents. How many mothers pause to consider the influence which they exert on their unborn offspring; how the infant's mental, moral and physical organism is affected by her conduct, even by her very thoughts and feelings. It is said a child is born happy or miserable, according to the state of its mother during pregnancy. Even its muscular structure may be made strong by proper food and exercise, or made weak and miserable by indolence or unsuitable diet. And how many fathers act their part well in the production of healthy, vigorous offspring? Too often the marriage rite is made a license of lust, and the most serious results follow the violation of sexual law. Such indulgence during gestation is a crime against nature and a sin against reason and conscience. It robs the child of its right to be well born, and perpetuates a diseased and perverted offspring.

Besides the ignorance regarding the principles of physiology and the development of human life, parents are careless and culpable respecting the care and management of infants. In vain are protesting voices raised against this unseen foe; in vain are essays and books written, each echoing in its pages the mournful fact that in this highly favored and prosperous land forty per cent. of our infants die before they reach the end of their second year, and this occurs largely through ignorance and mismanagement. This is a fearful mortality, and no one can believe that the Creator ever intended to nip in the bud nearly one-half of the infant population; enlightened reason rebels against such a conclusion. Nor is it that the mother does not try to care for her child, for the kindest feelings flow out instinctively towards her helpless offspring; but it is simply that she does not know *how to feed and take care of her baby.*

Life and health are not a mere matter of chance; no one is so well aware of this fact as the farmer and stock-raiser, who exercise the greatest care in the breeding of horses, cattle, sheep and even dogs. No cost nor pains are spared in the parentage of these, and with what care does he study the question of health, speed and endurance for the animal having a *moneyed* value; but when the question is that of " clothing an immortal soul in human form," the question of health and excellence is rarely considered. How unfortunate that mothers who have time to spare on all the frivolities of the day should so neglect these important matters, simply because it is unfashionable to inform themselves in regard to the origin and development of human life, and the means adapted by nature for its preservation.

It is said that every person born with a healthy constitution—free from the taint of disease—is responsible for his sickness. How then can disease be prevented? Simply by living, as far as possible, in accordance with all the conditions of health, avoiding all excesses that lead to exhaustion, and keeping up the strength and purity of the system. But, however strong we may feel, we must not uselessly expose ourselves to the pestilence that walketh in darkness. The way to prevent disease is to study and obey the laws of life.

These are not the only considerations that throw light on the origin of disease and lead to the conviction that, to a very great extent, we hold our health and life at will. "It is the fate of a great majority of our species," says an accomplished writer, "to fall from the hands of nature into those of an ignorant nurse and an *ignorant mother*. In all the departments of life in which *men* are called to act, some preparatory discipline is deemed necessary and afforded; but where women are concerned, the presiding deity is *chance*." She enters her guardianship helpless and alone, a prey to doubts and fears unparalleled in other relations of life. She is then kept in a state of painful alarm and apprehension by the occurrence of the most trifling circumstances, or allows real danger to steal on in a state of the most fatal, because unguarded, security.

The proper management of infants is, therefore, a subject of the utmost importance to every human being, and no mother can be too thoughtful, too refined, too highly gifted with knowledge for the important task of training and educating the rising generation.

Many are the efforts now being put forth to remedy the palpable defects in the prevailing systems of education, to purify the moral atmosphere and make the world better. Books are being written, philanthropic societies are being formed, and the most advanced thought uttered from pulpit and platform on all subjects pertaining to the highest faculties of life and the development of human character. Never at any time has the outlook for reform been so full of hope and inspiration—thanks to the Woman's Christian Temperance Union for much that has been done and is still being done by this noble band in the work of moral reform. It is educating public sentiment up to the highest standard of total abstinence; it is filling the hearts and homes with purer thoughts and bettering the condition of humanity everywhere. In the department of social purity it is making rapid strides, and besides protecting the weak it is teaching mothers the "sacredness of motherhood," and the best way of training their little ones that they may steer clear of the rocks and shoals upon which so many of the innocent and ignorant are being lost. To the reckless and wayward it extends a helping hand, and those who have already fallen it lifts up and encourages to do better. So we have every reason to be thankful to these "White Ribboners" for what they have already done and give promise of doing for "God and Home and Native Land."

A Closing Thought. — Looking, then, at the situation from whatever standpoint we may, the outlook is encouraging. And our closing thought to the reader is, having received from our parents, grandparents and great-grandparents a weak, puny, sickly, short-lived inheritance—which is the result of their transgressions—we find ourselves in discord with the harmonies of nature and living out of the Divine order. And now, if we would return to our wonted state of health and happiness; if we would be cured of this blood-poisoning—which has been handed down to us by our forefathers—then we must get in harmony with the laws of our being; and to do this the work must begin at home with ourselves. Every individual who lives in the conditions of health helps to make the world better; every man or woman who lives a pure virtuous life helps to remove badness, dishonesty, sensuality and drunkenness, and benefits the race; and if such persons would combine their purified and invigorated lives in the production of healthy offspring, they would confer an inestimable blessing upon universal humanity.

INDEX.

Abortion, 74
   criminal, 75
   methods of procuring, 78
   symptoms of, 74
Abuse of the sexual functions, 32
Advice to married people, 26
   to a young mother, 136
Air, impure, 61
After-birth, 90
Alcohol, evil effects of, 158
Alcoholic liquors, 167
   food puzzle, 162
   medication, 160
Baby, care of, 91
   chances to live, 111
   how to dress, 100
   how to feed, 125
   how to wash, 97
Baby's first meal, 131
   three meals a day, 120
Bad books, 210
Bathing, 58
Battle of life, 112
Best age to marry, 24
Book of nature, 152
Bribing children, 152
Candidates for matrimony, 11
Care of the infant, 91
   of the mother, 106
Catmint tea, 128
Cleanliness, 94
Cold, a cause of disease, 118
Colic of infants, 128
Confession of an opium slave, 192
Constipation, 71
   of infants, 117
Continence, 39
Cow's milk for babies, 138
Criminal abortion, 75
   abortion, remedy for, 85
Cutting the cord, 97
Death among infants, 115
Deception in courtship, 30
Dentition, 114, 142
Diaper, how to make, 103
Diet during pregnancy, 57
   for infants, 138
Disease without a name, 38
Diseases of pregnancy, 67
Dishonesty in love affairs, 19

Divers views on diet, 136
Dress for the baby, 101
Dressing the navel, 100
Duration of confinement, 108
   of pregnancy, 55
Dyspepsia of infants, 134
Early education, 149
Eating too much, 116
Everybody is sick, 7
Evil associations, 153
   effects of alcohol, 158
   effects of opium, 189
   effects of tobacco, 177
Evolution of fœtus, 44
Exercise, 63
Faulty alimentation, 115
Feeding and dosing, 125
Feet, swelling of, 72
Female weakness, 33
Fœticide, 75
Fœtus, development of, 47
   evolution of, 48
Generation, function of, 42
General conclusions, 215
Germ-cells, 42
Gestation, 50
Giving the baby food, 140
Hand-feeding of babies, 135
Happy homes, 154
Headache, 69
Health during pregnancy, 57
Heartburn, 69
Hemorrhoids, 70
Hints to young men, 24
   to young women, 22
Honesty the best policy, 20
How to dress the baby, 99
   to feed the baby, 125
   to save the baby, 109
   to wash the baby, 97
   to wean the baby, 141
Hungry cry, 126
Hygienic precautions, 57, 143
Impregnation, 44
Indifference, 29
Infant mortality, 111
Injections, vaginal, 108
Interests reciprocal, 28
Labor, parturition, 87
   position during, 88

224   INDEX.

Labor, premonitory symptoms, 89
License of lust, 36, 86
Lochia, 107
Love, passion of, 12
Masturbation, 201
Marrying for wealth, 21
Matrimonial, 11
    voyage, 26
Mental adaptation, 14
Milk, deficiency of, 122
    cow's, for baby, 138
    secretion of, 131
Miscarriage, 74
Morbid appetite, 133
Morning sickness, 68
Morphia, see Opium, 186
Mother, care of, 106
Mortality of infants, 111
Navel, how to dress, 100
Never marry a "dude," 24
New-born infant, 91
Nicotine, 177
Nurse, qualifications of, 92
Nursing the baby, 132
Obedience, 150
Obscene literature, 210
Opium, evil effects of, 189
    as a remedy, 188
    poisoning by, 189
    slave to, 192
Overfeeding the baby, 119
Pain in the side, 73
Passion of love, 12
Percentage of deaths, 112
Physical adaptation, 18
Piles, 70
Placenta, 90
Position for delivery, 88
    when taking food, 141
Pregnancy, 50
    signs of, 54
Preparation of cow's milk, 138
Primary cause of disease, 46
Prospective mother, 50
Pruritus vulva, 70
Purgative medicine, 107
Pure air, 94
Putting children to bed, 151
Reproduction of man, 42
Rest and sleep, 65
Scolding, 155

Secret vice, 201
    effects on vision, 206
    prevention of, 208
Self-abuse, 201
    cure for, 212
    effects on vision, 204
    evil effects of, 204
    prevention of, 208
    symptoms of, 202
Separate beds to sleep in, 41
Sexual indulgence during pregnancy, 52
    knowledge, 155
Shun the tobacco user, 23
    the tippler, 22
    the lustful man, 23
Signs of pregnancy, 54
Sleep, 66
Spermatozoa, 42
Sperm-cells, 42
Soothing syrup, 127
Starting right, 129
Stuffing and drugging, 126
Substitute for mother's milk, 138
Swelling of the feet, 72
Taking cold, 118
Teach obedience, 150
Teething sickness, 114
Temperature of room, 98
The breasts, 55
    child's primer, 152
    infant, 91
    lochia, 107
Three meals a day, 120
Tight lacing, 59
Tobacco, evil effects of, 177
    poisoning by, 145
    smoke, 143
To the reader, 5
Traditional notions, 60
Value of a smile, 30
Varicose veins, 72
Ventilation, 63
Washing the baby, 97
Waterbrash, 68
Weaning the baby, 141
What constitutes abuse, 36
Wheat gruel, 139
Where did baby come from? 156
Who suffers? 34

www.ingramcontent.com/pod-product-compliance
Lightning Source LLC
Chambersburg PA
CBHW022016220426
43663CB00007B/1098